FREIGHT WAGONS and LOADS

in service on the

GREAT WESTERN RAILWAY

and

BRITISH RAIL, WESTERN REGION

G
3226
10 TONS TARE 5.6
W
45748

FREIGHT WAGONS and LOADS

in service on the

GREAT WESTERN RAILWAY

and

BRITISH RAIL, WESTERN REGION

by

J. H. Russell

Oxford Publishing Co.

ISBN 0 86093 155 2

A FOULIS-OPC Railway Book

© 1981 J.H. Russell & Oxford Publishing Co.
Reprinted 1989

Published by:
Haynes Publishing Group
Sparkford, Near Yeovil, Somerset. BA22 7JJ.

Haynes Publications Inc.
861 Lawrence Drive, Newbury Park, California 91320, USA.

Printed by: J.H. Haynes & Co.Ltd

INTRODUCTION

This work is concerned with railway wagons generally, and in particular those which could have been seen at work on the old Great Western Railway which later became the Western Region of British Rail.

The necessity of moving heavy materials from one place to another has always created problems for mankind. Our Stone Age ancestors dragged the loads over the ground on sledges or moved huge slabs of rock by means of rollers crudely hacked from trees. The invention of the wheel revolutionised transportation and the first primitive rollers gave way to discs of timber mounted on an axle which enabled a load to be hauled or pushed a greater distance. From this humble beginning, it was a short step to a box with a pair of wheels at each end, and from there it was found that if wooden rails were provided for the wheels to run upon, friction was decreased and rolling resistance lessened even further.

The need for moving coal in the mines in the sixteenth century caused wooden rails for flangeways to be laid, so that trams loaded with coal could be pushed and hauled from the coal face to the mine entrance, often by women and small children. When it was realized that a metal wheel would roll on a metal rail with even less effort, the age of the railway was born and this contributed in no small way to the Industrial Revolution of the seventeenth century.

Horses which had taken the place of manpower, were themselves superseded by the steam locomotive which quickly proved itself capable of moving strings or trains of wagons along a specially laid railway, and so, from the slow laborious hauling of road vehicles along wagonways and the dragging of barges along the canals, a system of quick, efficient and safe movement of every kind of merchandise was established. This in turn has led to the fast freight trains of 1,000 tons and more moving around the world's railways at speeds of up to 100 m.p.h.

Although the conveyance of passengers by train has always been more in the public eye than the less conspicuous movement of freight, the latter did, and still does, make a greater contribution to the Railway exchequer! and has to me as an ex-railwayman, been of greater interest. The Railway companies of the United Kingdom were 'Common Carriers' which meant that, by Act of Parliament, any form of merchandise, from coal to cattle, or from meat to machinery, just had to be transported on demand and therefore, to accommodate this necessity, vehicles of every type, size and shape were constructed over the years at the railway factories.

The very diversity of design has always intrigued me and I have made a collection of photographs to illustrate just how many of the widely differing loads were handled on the Great Western Railway. This then is the raison d'etre of this work. Three previous books dealing with vehicles belonging solely to the Great Western Railway have been produced, but I wanted to show as many types of freight vehicles as possible, designed for or actually transporting their specific traffic over the past century.

It is a source of wonder to me that such a mundane subject as railway wagons can prove of interest to readers, but as experience has shown, there still appears to be a great demand for further information of any kind to do with railways and their handling of traffic. I humbly offer this collection hoping it will answer some questions, pose others, and find a place on the already crowded shelves of fellow enthusiasts.

J. H. Russell
July 1981

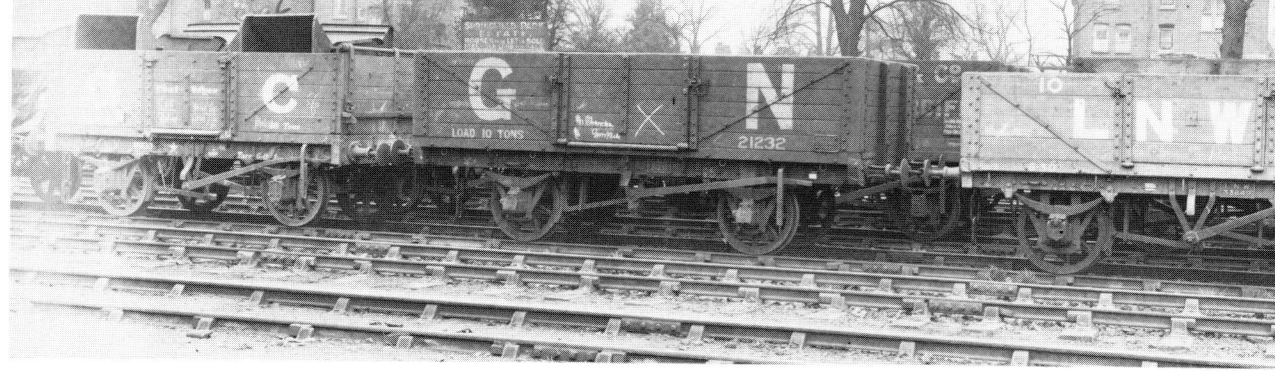

This opening page illustrates seven styles of STANDARD wagons as built by seven different railway companies before the grouping of 1923. In **Figure 1** on the left is a long Open 'C' of the Great Western Railway, in the centre stands a round ended 10 ton open fitted with a sheet bar and belonging to the London, South Western Railway, running number 3471. On the right of the picture is a seven plank open No. 75907 produced at the Derby factory of the Midland Railway.

Figure 1

Figure 2

Figure 2 shows a 10 ton coal wagon of the Great Central Railway fitted with an end door at one end only, the number of the vehicle being 18630. Next to this wagon is a 6 plank, 10 ton open of the Great Northern Railway No. 21232 built at Doncaster and at the right end of the picture is a 4 plank version of the 10 ton capacity open, as built by the London and North Western Railway at Wolverton, No. 33849.

Figure 3

Figure 3 portrays a 10 ton covered wagon of the Caledonian Railway fitted with cross bracing and a sliding door. All these vehicles were part of a train being marshalled at Acton on the Great Western Railway in 1920.

Figure 4.

Open wagons were built in various sizes ranging from those with but a single plank high to large vehicles with as many as seven planks on edge. This illustration depicts a small three plank open of 8 tons capacity, loaded with carboys of acid. Note how the glass jars were themselves in containers which were then packed in straw to avoid breakages.

Wagon No. 34920 was fitted with grease axle boxes and had a brake on one side only. Two similar vehicles, but with four planks, can be seen at top left, this was No. 71375 which had a capacity of 10 tons. The vacuum brakes covered van in the top centre is one of the ventilated series and is No. 82081.

W
71375
G W
VENTILATED VAN
82081
G W
34920
8 Tons. Tare 4-13

Apart from the basic loads of coal and timber, the Great Western Railway also carried many other consignments in large quantities, and one of these I knew well when starting as a lad on the Great Western Railway was hay for cattle and horse fodder. Nowadays hay is cut in the fields and baled immediately into oblong cubes, but before the advent of the baler, hay was stacked in ricks in the farmyard and only when sold or required for use, would a labourer with a large hay knife attack the rick and cut the hay into oblong trusses. These were then transported to the railway yard on road wagons drawn by horses and loaded by the railway staff onto the railway wagons.

In order to make a safe load for travelling, a certain method of stacking had to be observed and this had to be learnt by lad apprentices, i.e. myself. These four photographs, **Figure 5, Figure 6, Figure 7** and **Figure 8** show a quartet of various vehicles commandeered for hay loading. **Figure 5** is of a seven-plank open of the Great Eastern Railway, No. 9015, and like all the other three in the series, shows the load ready for sheeting and roping. **Figure 6** depicts a four-plank open of the Caledonian Railway, No. 70820.

Figure 5

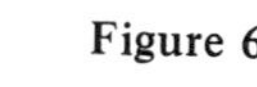

Figure 6

Figure 7

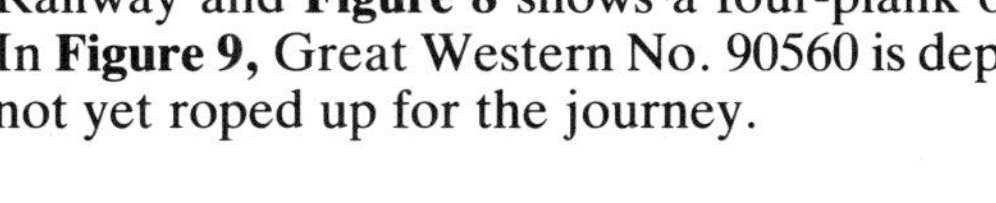

Figure 8

Figure 9

Figure 7 is a picture of No. 39679, a small three-plank open of the Great Western Railway and **Figure 8** shows a four-plank open No. 72568 fitted with a sheet bar. In **Figure 9,** Great Western No. 90560 is depicted with the wagon sheets in place but not yet roped up for the journey.

Taken in 1912, the photograph on this page, **Figure 10,** is of a standard four-plank open, loaded with large pit props and is stacked in such a way as to travel safely without the need for a check wagon or other restraint other than the one rope at one end. The shunter is moving the wagon with a pinch bar in order to couple to the adjoining wagon.

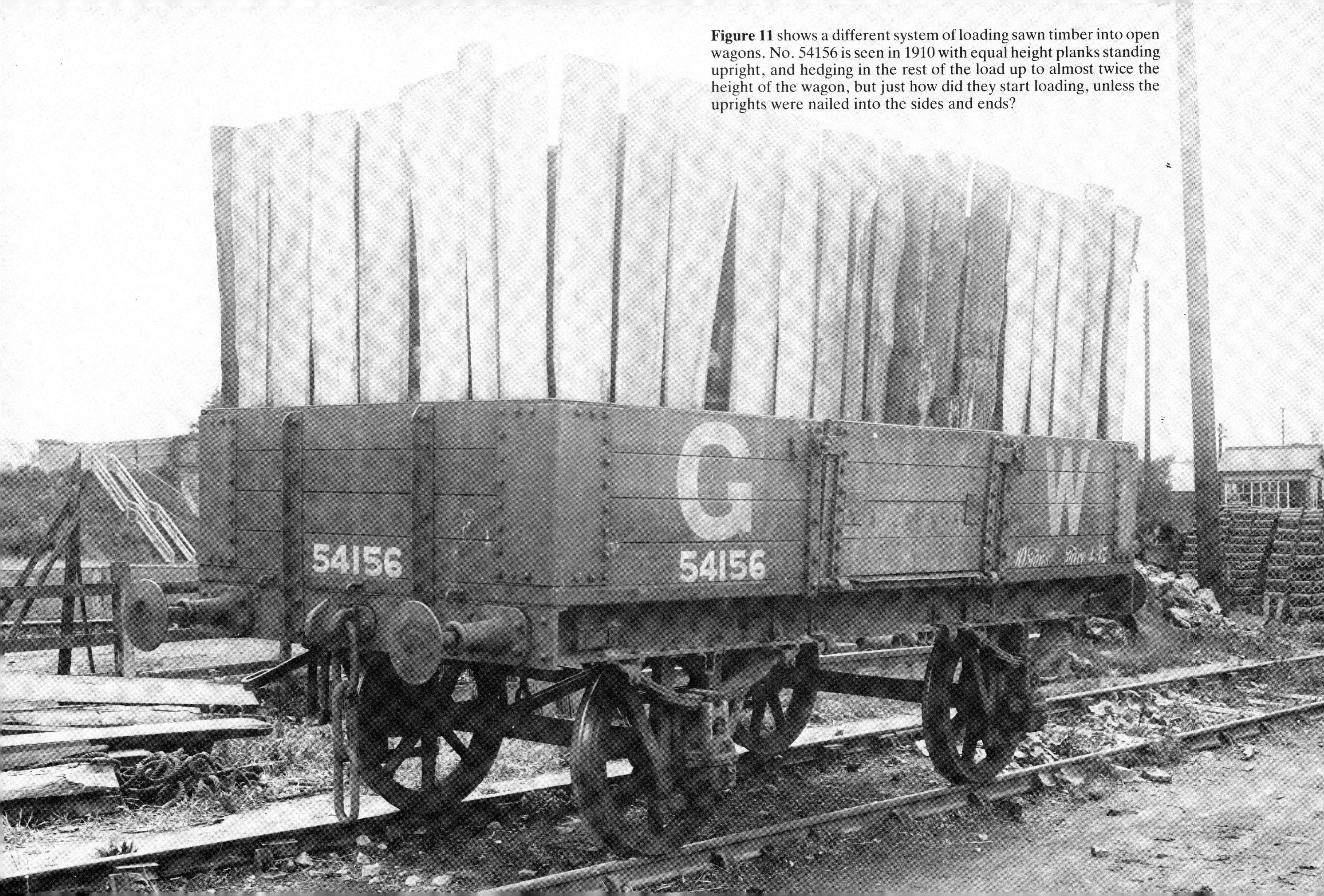

Figure 11 shows a different system of loading sawn timber into open wagons. No. 54156 is seen in 1910 with equal height planks standing upright, and hedging in the rest of the load up to almost twice the height of the wagon, but just how did they start loading, unless the uprights were nailed into the sides and ends?

Figure 12

Figure 13

The upper illustration (**Figure 12**) is of a 12 ton capacity five-plank open of the Great Western Railway as built at Swindon on 9th May, 1934. As can be seen, the number is 122696 constructed to Diagram 0.31 on Lot 1131. Fitted with disc wheels and long handle brakes, this vehicle had the old type end stanchions. **Figure 13** (*right*) shows No. 18364, an earlier 10 ton five-plank open fitted with spoked wheels and short buffer shanks. The photograph was taken in January of 1937 when the vehicle was reconditioned. It makes a good comparison with the vehicle above. There are many differences – the buffer beams are tapered at the ends, the door guards are set closer together than with No. 122696, and note that the extra wide plank is at the top of the wagon, whereas in No. 122696 it is second up from the wagon floor. This vehicle also has the Great Western Railway 'either side' brake.

This photograph (**Figure 14**) was taken at Swindon Goods yard on 24th October, 1922, to show faulty loading of sawn timber en route from Brentford Docks. As can be seen, the load is loosely roped and in danger of dropping off should heavy shunting occur. The wagon is No. R491, one of the many six-plank, 12 ton capacity high-sided opens of the North Eastern Railway, built at Darlington.

Figure 15. North Eastern Railway wagon No. R491 again, showing the opposite side of the vehicle with the very loose ropes which are not securing the load in any way, and also the large overhang which necessitated a check wagon to be used underneath this projecting timber.

Figure 16 shows the end view of the timber load in North Eastern Railway six-plank open wagon No. R491. This shows clearly how close the pieces of timbers were to the top of the wagon and so in danger of being thrown off at great danger to railway operating in general.

Figure 17

POWELL'S T...LLERY STEAM COAL Cº
(Limited)
CARDIFF
Nº 1135
Empty to
Abertillery G.W.R.
Tare 5. 16. 0
John P. Hacquoil & Cº
General Managers
Load 10 Tons

Figure 18

Figure 17 shows a privately owned five-plank open wagon being used to convey round timber. Four pieces of the load were placed upright, the remainder of the lumber being set between these spaces to utilize the extra height gained. As can be seen, the vehicle used was owned by Powell's Tillery Steam Coal Co. and was No. 1135. Obviously the timbers were to be used as pit props in the South Wales Colliery system.

The conveyance of china clay from Fowey in Cornwall caused many wagons to suffer from wet rot of the floor planks and it was therefore decided to fit many of the open wagons used for this freight with zinc sheets on the bed of the vehicle. A further advantage of the metal sheeting on the floor of the wagon was the ease of emptying when the end tipplers were used to off-load the clay at the docks. **Figure 19** shows one of this series, No. P270732 in 1952, photographed at Swindon. In **Figure 18** the end door of No. P270732 is opened to allow the zinc-lined floor to be seen clearly.

Figure 19

Figure 20

Figure 21

The china clay trade at Fowey was, and still is, quite extensive and the port and harbour installations complicated and interesting. So much so that several pages here have been devoted to this traffic and how the clay was handled at the jetties. **Figure 20** illustrates one system of emptying through the end doors. The wagon was secured to the tipper platform, the door catches unlatched and one end of the platform was raised by means of a wheeled track on the girder tower, astride the siding. **Figure 21** shows the pivoted platform method of unloading. Electrically powered, the platform forming part of the siding is balanced centrally and once the wagon is secured thereon, the tipper pivots and so unloads the clay from the wagon.

This old photograph (**Figure 22**) with the three-masted sailing ship alongside the jetty shows clearly the action of the pivoted tippler table. From the bottom of the table, the clay passed up a conveyor belt, and finally dropped into the holds of the ship waiting alongside.

The next four illustrations (**Figures 23, 24, 25 and 26**) depict the quay facilities at Fowey in the 1925 period, and are self explanatory.

Figure 23

Figure 24

Figure 25

Figure 26

W 94071
94071
9/53
9/52

The photograph above was made specially for the china clay traffic at Fowey and was a series of wagons built under diagram MWOT of British Rail and **Figure 27** illustrates No. W94071, one of this zinc floored pattern, but also fitted with an internal sheet bar. **Figure 28** shows the end door of No. W94071 and gives the reason for the sheet bar being located on the inside of the wagon. Note that sheet ties have changed from the older hemp rope variety to the modern leather strap slotting through plate loops screwed to the wagon planks.

Wagon No. W94004 seen in **Figure 29** is another of the earlier vehicles which was reconditioned for the china clay traffic in 1950. This vehicle was originally built on Lot 777 to Diagram O.13. Note the white diagonal stripe which was painted to indicate the end door part of the vehicle.

Figure 30 shows No. B743096, one of the wagons built at Swindon in 1955, especially for the china clay traffic at St. Blazey.

Figure 31 is a photograph of wagon No. DW280, another reconditioned vehicle utilized for the carriage of locomotive wheels from Swindon factory to outstations all over the Western Region system.
Originally built on Lot 218 to diagram 0.22, this conversion was dated 1953 and consisted of having the floor specially strengthened and retained checks installed.

Figure 32 shows another modification to an original design. Wagon No. W143449 was one of the 0.37 diagram series from Lot 1379, and in 1951 steel girders replaced the original bottom two end planks of the vehicle. This was thought necessary as the loading of steel bars into open wagons was resulting in great damage to the two lower planks, due to heavy shunting causing the load to break through the wagon end.

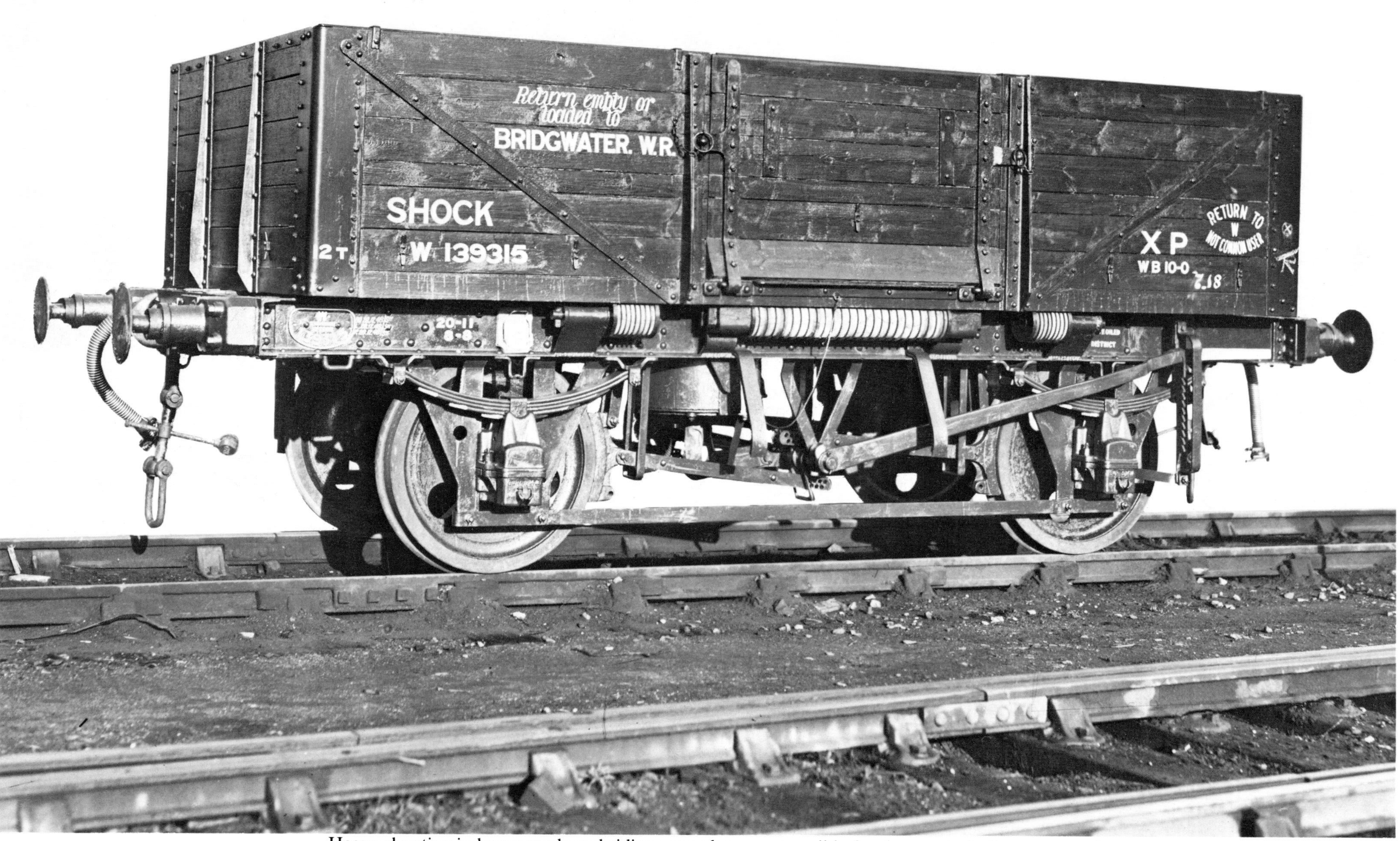

Heavy shunting in hump yards and sidings was always responsible for damage to both wagons and load, and many systems were tried to ease this problem. One of the most successful was the separating of the wagon body from the underframe and fitting of rubber shock absorbers which allowed the loaded body to slide slightly and to absorb the impact of shunting movements. **Figure 33** shows No. W139315,

Figure 34 shows No. W139308, taken in August 1954 and is the same design of wagon as **Figure 33.** To make the vehicle more easily identifiable to shunters and train crews, these vehicles were painted bauxite brown with three white upright stripes on each side of the wagon.

Several of the 0.44 series of shock-absorbing open wagons were fitted with a sheet supporting bar so that a load requiring to be kept dry could have a sheet covering the whole wagon and the bar when erected would raise the wagon sheet like the ridge pole of a tent and so shed the rain off the load. **Figure 35** shows No. W139359 with the bar dropped down out of harm's way.

Figure 23 illustrates No. B721312 built for the Western Region at Ashford works of the Southern Region in 1954, but with the sheet supporting bar in the upright position. Note the different placing of the painted stripe. Readers have asked the reason for the triangle plate fixed on the upright of the bar. This was fitted to fill the gap left when a square wagon sheet was resting on the bar and pulled down on to the wagon sides.

A development of the sheeted open wagon design was carried out in 1964 when steel traffic coming into the country at the docks was required to be conveyed to various mills around the country. **Figure 37** depicts No. B457615, one of the 13 ton capacity drop sided opens fitted with a three bar supporter and a nylon sheet which always stayed with the vehicle. Official photograph taken at Swindon in May 1964.

Figure 38 is an interesting photograph as it shows one of the steel coil wagons, which was converted from a 30 ton pig iron vehicle. This wagon was used for conveying steel strip and coil from steel mills to factories. Wagon No. B744681 was posed for this photograph and had the special treatment of the white sheet holders behind the vehicle. These photographic assistants held these screens behind the running gear so that the detail of the underframe was not lost amongst background items.

Figure 39

M.o.T. 33011
16 TONS
7·13·0
P. 3·48
L. 3·48

Figure 39 is a fine official photograph of one of the numerous mineral wagons made for the Ministry of Transport in March 1948. Constructed entirely of steel, the carrying capacity was 16 tons and had many modern features. The end door, made from a single steel pressing, was hinged from a heavy lintel of deep section, heavily gusseted and obviously designed for hard usage. The side doors were in two sections, the larger lower dropping on to a single retainer, and the small upper flap door, opening over the cross member, which divided the two doors.

Two of the long open wagons are featured on this page, which in Great Western days were coded as 'Open C'. **Figure 40** in the upper photograph shows No. B731085 and is an obvious descendant of the original Great Western Railway design, with four wooden planks on the sides and ends, and a heavy frame mounted on to a 19′ 6″ wheelbase. The diagram was 0.47 to Lot 2127 and the carrying capacity was 22 tons. **Figure 41** shows the 1953 version of the 'tube' wagon built at Swindon on Lot 2209. Note that the wheelbase has been shortened to 17′6″ and the ends are now of corrugated steel.

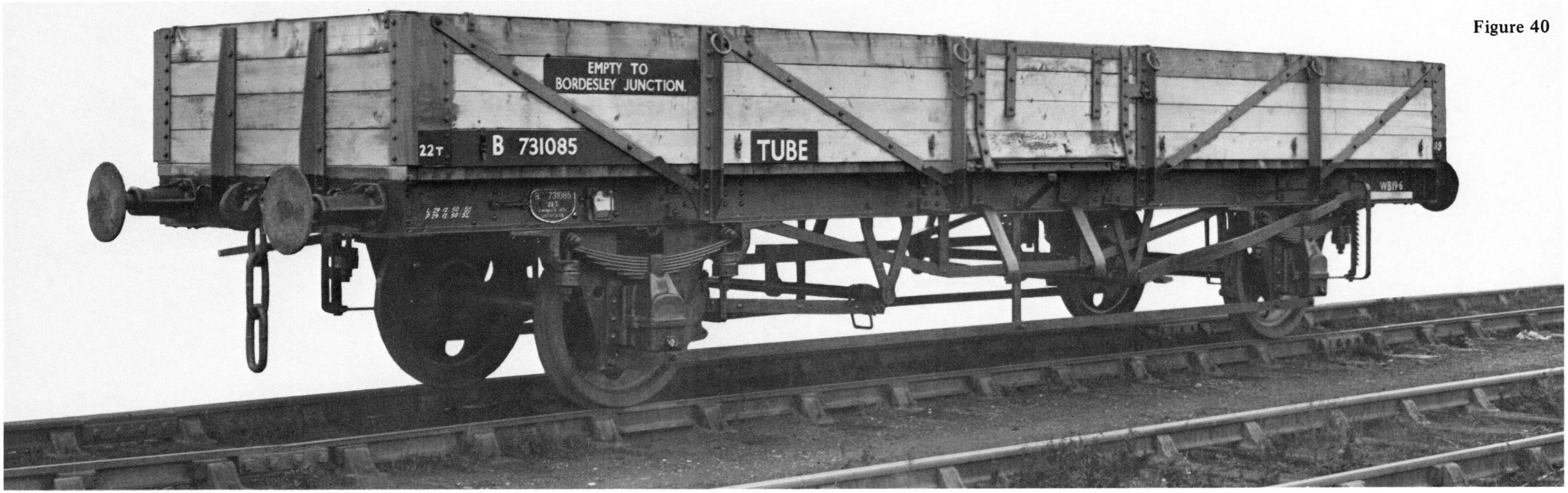

Figure 40

Figure 41

Figure 42

Figure 42 is another 'pipe' wagon built at Swindon in 1953. This was a 12 ton vehicle fitted with spring loaded double doors on each side. As well as both doors being capable of dropping right down, the centre door post could be lifted out of its socket and also lowered out of the way. This enabled the entire wagon side to be cleared to facilitate loading of long pipes or tubes from the side. The wagon was No. B740652 and was part of Lot 2329.

Figure 43 shows a special wagon constructed at Swindon in 1962. No. DW42187 was designed for use with the breakdown vans. The open top part of the body was used for wooden packing, slings, chains and similar gear necessary for accident work, whilst the lower three hatches were used for heavy items which could be unloaded close down to the track such as re-railing irons, levers and cables. Re-stowage was also much easier as the height of the hatches above rail level was very small. Fitted with train braking and screw couplings, these wagons could run at express speeds.

Figure 43

Coils of steel wire were always a heavy freight, and **Figure 44** shows one of the four plank wagons of the Great Western Railway loaded with this form of traffic in 1913. No. 50815 had a 10 ton capacity and was fitted with a sheet bar. The axle boxes were of the grease lubrication type and a hand brake on one side only away from the side shown in the photograph.
One further point to make in this picture, the siding track on which the wagon stands is the early type with the wooden keys fitted on the inside of the rail rather than the better known style of having the keys outside the rail.

Figure 45

Figure 46

Figure 45 (upper photograph) — Wagon No. B949000 was one of the bogie open wagons which were made at Swindon in 1950 for the conveyance of steel strip in coils from the South Wales steel mills. Capable of a 42 ton load, they ran on a pair of Great Western Railway style heavy bogies with hand brakes on either side working on one bogie each. The diagram was 0.46 and the Lot was 2209 of 1950.

Figure 46 (lower photograph) shows a modification of the 0.46 series when several vehicles were fitted with vacuum brakes and screw couplings and so could be marked up as X.P. (High Speed Running). No. B949007 seen at Swindon in 1958 is one of the series so fitted.

Figure 47 is an excellent photograph taken at Swindon in 1910 of two types of 'loco' coal wagons. No. 43699 was one of the Diagram N2 design built in 1905, having a capacity of 20 tons built to Lot 481. The other wagon was one of the 40 ton bogie vehicles built on the N14 design, No. 53993. Both wagons were loaded with coke in this picture at the gas works at Swindon. Many readers have raised the question of the painting of 'loco' wagons and I would state categorically that in the time that I was with the Great Western Railway, all these departmental vehicles labelled 'loco' were painted black all over, with lettering all white.

Figure 48

In the year 1936 the General Manager of the Great Western Railway, Felix Pole, was instrumental in sponsoring the use of 20 ton mineral wagons to replace the then multitudinous 'private owner' 10 and 12 ton wagons. These were in common use for the conveyance of coal from pit to coal merchants' siding. **Figure 48** was taken to show a comparison between one of the new all steel 20 ton wagons and the 12 ton wooden vehicle No. 1880 of Messrs. Bradbury of London. Special inducements were offered in freight costings but only the largest collieries took up the option and consequently hired the steel wagons from the Great Western Railway.

Figure 49 shows several varieties of Great Western Railway 'loco' coal wagons, all loaded with the special Welsh steam coal, which was the staple fuel of the Swindon locomotives. No. 83187 is nearest the camera and three different designs of steel wagons are in line ahead.

Figure 49

Figure 50

Figure 51

Two 'loco' coal wagons feature on this page, but with totally different services. No. 33156 was one of the N27 series (built on Lot 1260) of 20 ton capacity, with four side doors only (**Figure 50**). This vehicle's function was for conveying steam coal from South Wales to the various locomotive sheds for off loading on the coal stages into the tenders of the engines. The 20 ton hopper wagon, No. 83998 in **Figure 51** is one of a batch of 25 which were built between 1923–7 on Lot 917 to Diagram N25. As constructed they were fitted with vacuum brake, but several, including No. 83998, had this gear removed. These vehicles worked between Swindon factory gas works and Wath Main colliery, Barnsley, conveying small gas coal for feeding the retorts at the work's gas plant.

GWR
SALVAGE
SAVE FOR VICTORY
GWR
10T
47305
6-8

Towards the end of 1940, England was at war with Germany and due to heavy losses in merchant shipping and consequent shortage of many vital materials including paper, many salvage drives were started to re-cycle waste. Towards this end the Great Western Railway converted two old goods vans (Iron Minks) so that these vehicles could tour the system and collect all waste paper for re-pulping. The two wagons concerned were Nos. 47305 and 47528, both to the design of V6, of which there were more than 4,000 made. **Figure 52** illustrates 47305 in a three quarter view, and note that the hand brake on the side nearest camera operates only one brake block, that on the opposite side. The usual two brakes on the two sides are not interconnected.

Figure 53 shows No. 47528, slightly different from the previous wagon in having two double block brakes, one on each side. The only other variation was in the painting. On No. 47305 the roundel was straw yellow and on No. 47528 it was painted white.

Photographed on the last day of 1933, **Figure 54** shows one of the bogie 'Iron Minks', built in 1912 to Diagram V1 (second batch).
These vehicles were equipped with vacuum brakes and heavy freight bogies, as they were designed for use on the night express freight trains. The capacity of this vehicle was 30 tons. Many of these vans were branded to ensure they remained on one particular route schedule, and as can be seen, No. 79599 worked between Paddington and Bristol.

Covered vans were many and various on the Great Western Railway and although not as numerous as the open wagons, nevertheless, many thousands were built at Swindon, not only by the old Great Western Railway Company, but also by British Rail Engineering.

Figure 55 depicts No. 123522, one of the ventilated vans, built to Diagram V23 on Lot 1125. Between the years of 1933 and 1941 more than 6,000 were built, some fitted with vacuum brakes and 'instanter' couplings, as with this example. Painted lead grey all over except for white roof and lettering.

There were 2,389 similar vehicles built to Diagram V23, which were also constructed over the same period of time as the previous wagon V23. **Figure 56** shows one of these photographed at Swindon in 1933. No. 123254 is very similar in design to the V23, the exception being the hand brake system. In this design, only two brake blocks are used, one on each wheel, both on one side only. Also this van was in common use, whereas in the previous illustration, No. 123522 is branded as a 'Not common user'.

Figure 57. A 4-wheeled ventilated van on a 9 foot wheelbase, No. 123001 was one of 936 similar wagons built on Lot 999, between 1927–9, to Diagram V21. This photograph was taken at Swindon on 18th January, 1933.

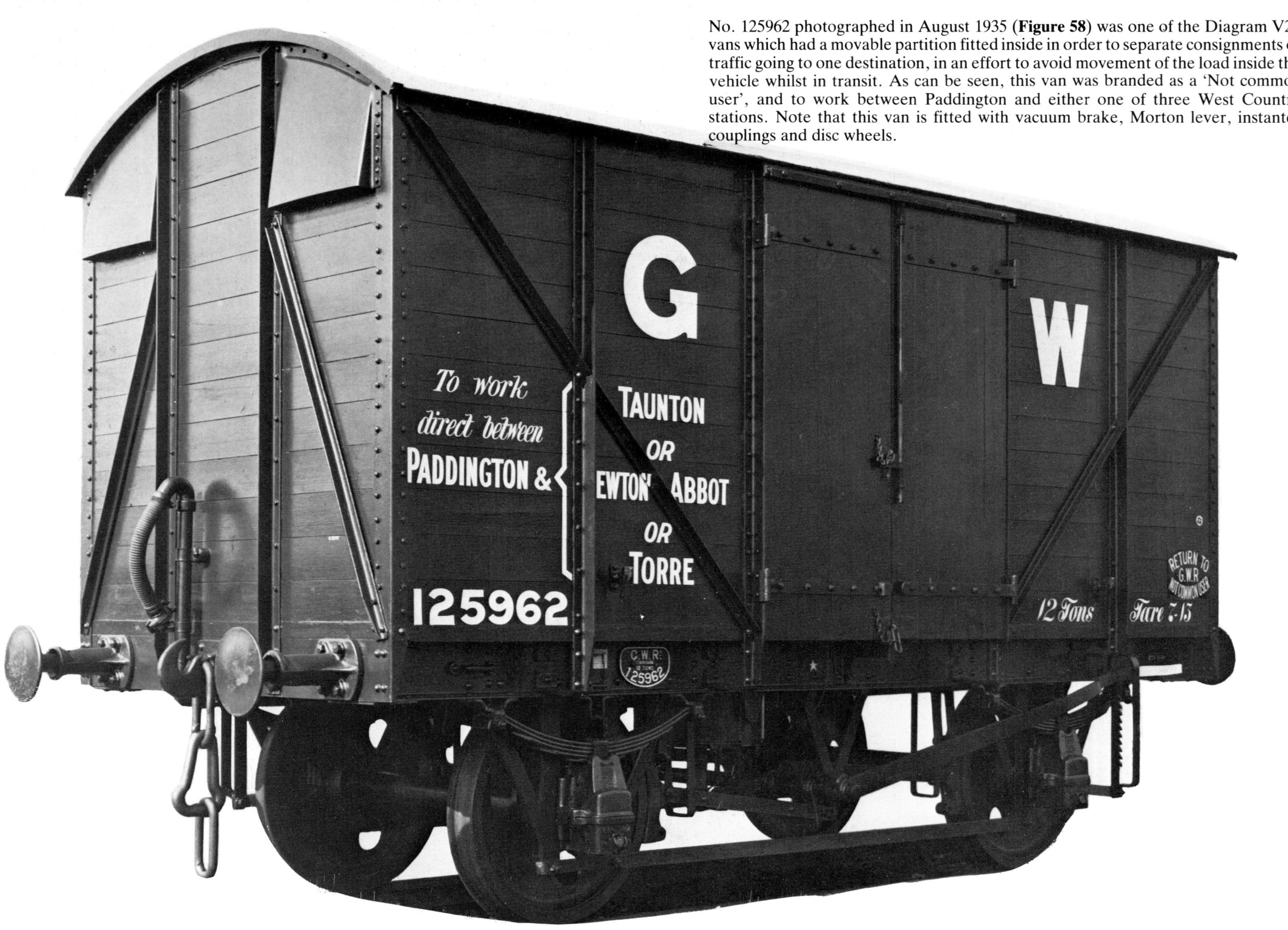

No. 125962 photographed in August 1935 (**Figure 58**) was one of the Diagram V23 vans which had a movable partition fitted inside in order to separate consignments of traffic going to one destination, in an effort to avoid movement of the load inside the vehicle whilst in transit. As can be seen, this van was branded as a 'Not common user', and to work between Paddington and either one of three West Country stations. Note that this van is fitted with vacuum brake, Morton lever, instanter couplings and disc wheels.

Figure 59 illustrates another branded van, one of the wagons also fitted with internal partitions. This was No. 126854 built to Diagram V26 and ordered on Lot 1209. Built in January 1937. Note the photographer's assistants holding the white screen behind the underframe, also look out for the hooped horse-drawn cart loaded on to the trolley wagon on the left.

Figure 60. Photographed at the factory in July 1938, No. 134054 is one of the V23 diagram ventilated vans, and was chosen to show the new style of lettering that was applied to freight stock in that year. Note that this van has screw-couplings and the vacuum hose in the lower position. The Lot was 1269.

Another of the V26 design is shown in **Figure 61** and shows a ventilated van on 10 foot wheelbase. Built and photographed in June 1940, No. 134089 was also fitted with internal movable partitions, and to identify this facility, these vehicles were branded 'PARTO'. The Lot was 1359.

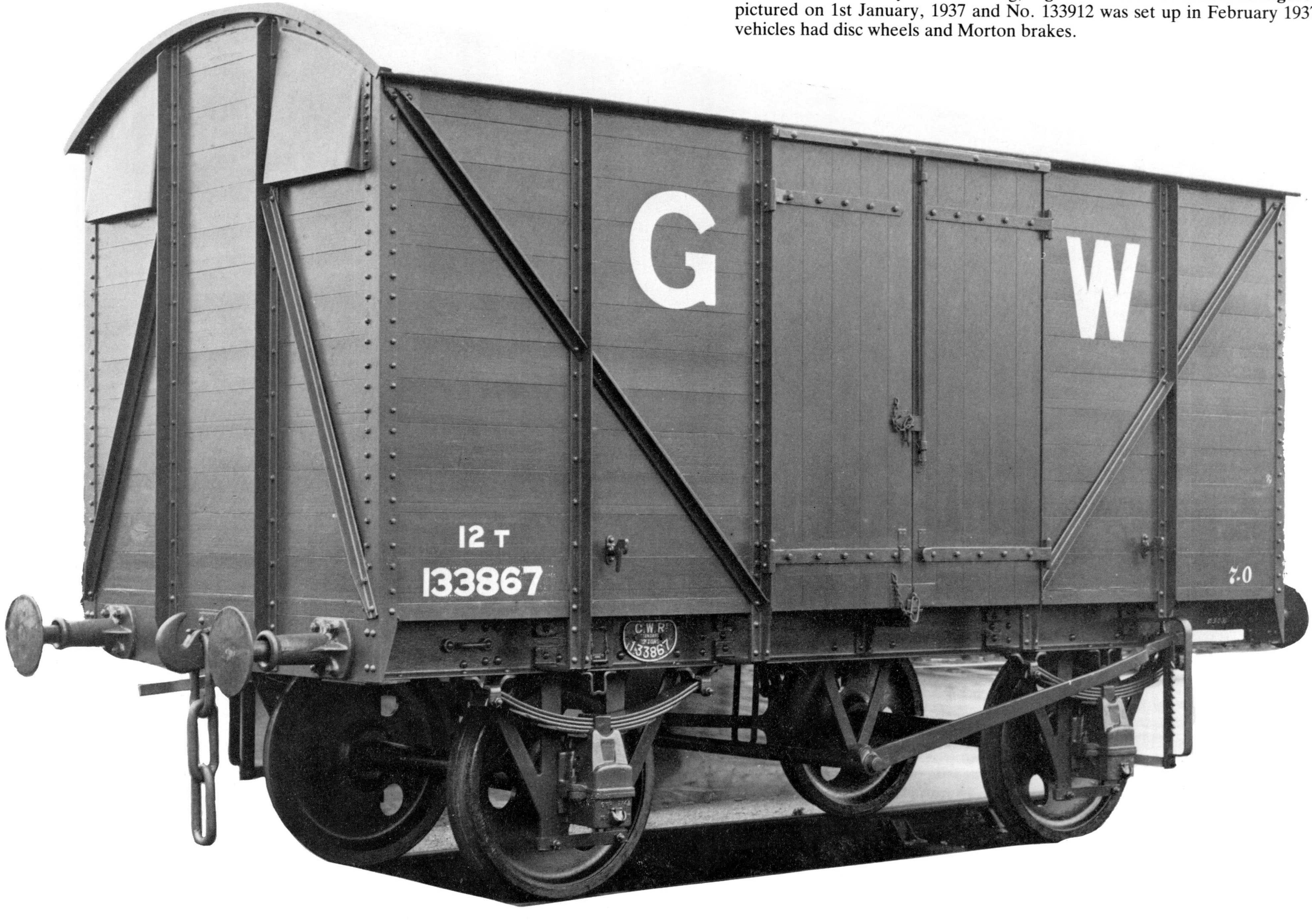

Two ventilated vans, both of the V24 diagram, photographed one month apart to show the different styles of lettering, **Figures 62–63.** No. 133867 in **Figure 62** was pictured on 1st January, 1937 and No. 133912 was set up in February 1937. Both vehicles had disc wheels and Morton brakes.

Figure 63

Figure 64 shows a ventilated van No. 112788 branded to work between Barnstaple and Paddington. This was one of the V26 design, built in 1937 and fitted with internal movable partitions. Disc wheels were fitted, together with vacuum brake and 'instanter' links.

No. 125581 in **Figure 65** was one of the first shock-absorbing ventilated vans, built in 1937 to try and solve the problem of damage to freight caused by heavy shunting. This particular vehicle was the one-off prototype and as such was given the Diagram V27 all to itself. All other similar vans differed slightly in being fitted with internal partitions.

Figure 66 shows the initial shock-absorbing van No. 125581 in three-quarter view, as opposed to the broadside angle seen in the previous study. This illustrates the rubber block shock absorbers and the special buffers quite well.

The success of the experimental shock-absorbing van led to the construction of a further 105 similar wagons, built between 1937 and 1940. These were slightly different from the prototype vehicle in having wooden partitions fitted inside to further reduce oscillation of loads during transit. Many of these ventilated vans were branded to work between specified depots. No. 139576 shown on this page (**Figure 67**) is an example, built to Diagram V28 for Lots 1297 and 1358.

During the war years 1941 to 1945, Swindon factory built 1,200 standard 12 ton non-vacuum ventilated vans to the design of V34 on order of Lot 1412, for general usage. As can be seen by No. 145759 in **Figure 68**, this was a straightforward Great Western pattern, using all standard fittings. Brake handles were on both sides, but brake shoes were only fitted on one side of the vehicle.

At first glance this ventilated van in **Figure 69** seems to be out of context, but it does have a place in this work. Between the years 1942 and 1943, 650 vans of 12 ton capacity were ordered on Great Western Railway Lot 1430 to Diagram V35 and built by the Southern Railway at Ashford and elsewhere. No. 144888 depicts one of the series, photographed at Swindon to show damage to one end caused by a shifted load. Although many of the fittings are pure Great Western Railway, the body of the vehicle is obviously of Southern origin.

Figure 70

Wartime shortage of seasoned timber prompted the use of other materials as substitutes in the construction of railway wagons. One of the many such alternatives was heavy duty plywood. **Figure 70** shows one of the ventilated vans built to the Diagram V37 in 1948 on Lot No. 1525. Note that although the upright angle-iron framing is bolted through the body plywood, the diagonals are not; being welded at top and bottom only.

Figure 71. Built in 1939 to Lot 1358, No. 139594 passed into British Rail ownership in 1948 and received the prefix 'W' to indicate this. Photographed in 1949 to illustrate the experimental painting which was being tried to make identification of these 'Shock vans' slightly easier, three white stripes were painted on each door and on the left-hand side of each end, and indeed were readily spotted amongst a train of similar vehicles. This particular wagon was branded 'Return empty or loaded to Gwalia T.P. Works, Briton Ferry, W.R.'

At first glance, this ventilated van (**Figure 72**) would appear to be identical to that in **Figure 70,** but there are slight differences. Constructed on Lot 2083 in 1950 to Diagram V38, the vehicle No. B753427 has spoked wheels in contrast to the three hole discs of W146243 and is fitted with wooden panels for label attachment. The roof has only one rain strip over the doors in place of the three on V37 which covered the length of the wagon.

Figure 73 illustrates the combination of the 'plywood' series of ventilated vans, with 'shock absorbing' vehicles designed at Swindon. Dated July 1958, this photograph shows No. B850333 built at the Western Region for use on the London Midland Region and branded 'Empty to Burton-on-Trent', used one supposes for beer traffic. Note the white painted stripes have now been spaced wider apart than the experimental style in **Figure 71.** This series was built on Lot 2158 and was fitted with label boards.

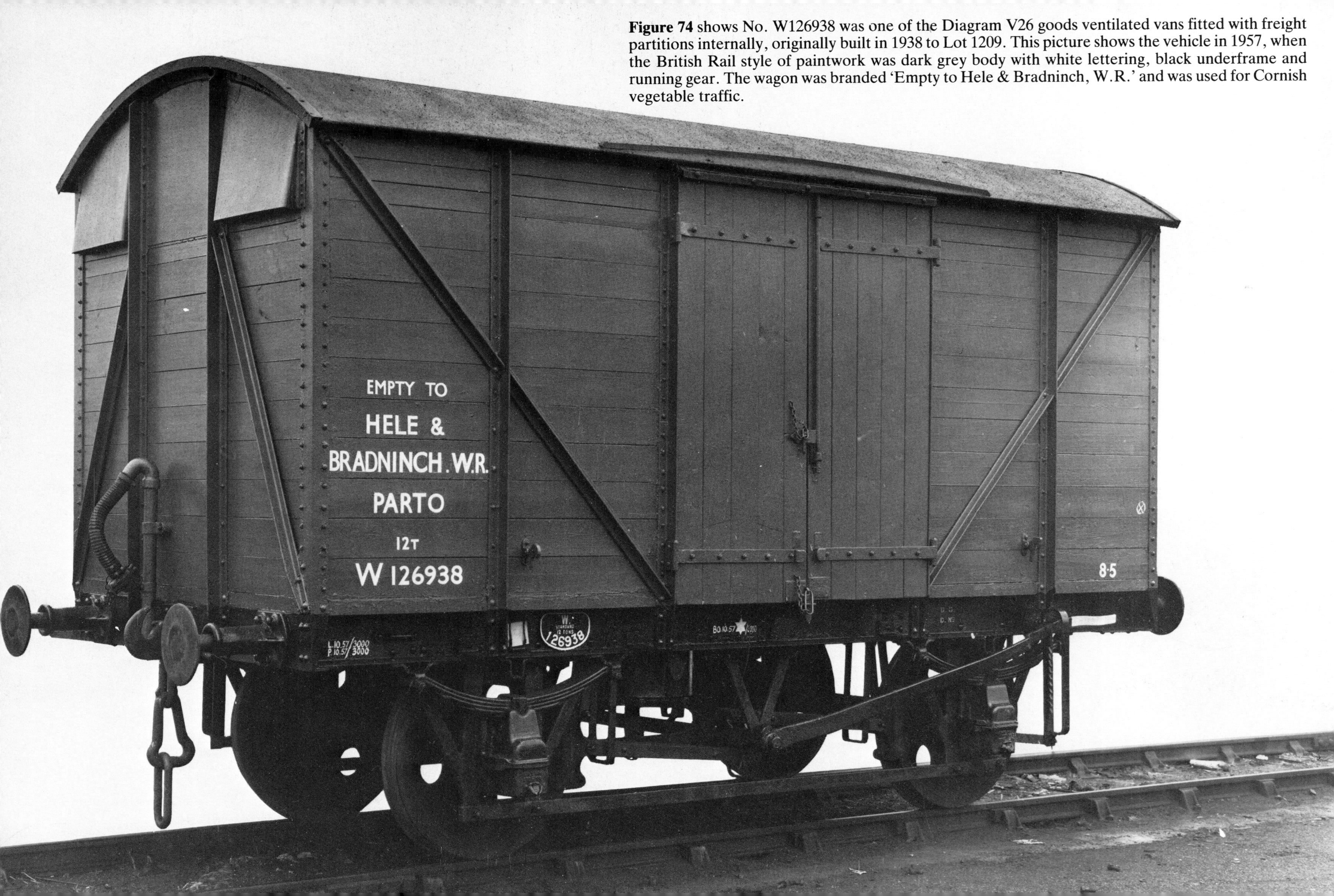

Figure 74 shows No. W126938 was one of the Diagram V26 goods ventilated vans fitted with freight partitions internally, originally built in 1938 to Lot 1209. This picture shows the vehicle in 1957, when the British Rail style of paintwork was dark grey body with white lettering, black underframe and running gear. The wagon was branded 'Empty to Hele & Bradninch, W.R.' and was used for Cornish vegetable traffic.

Figure 75 again shows the combining of railway designs. This ventilated · van built in 1959, one of many constructed to Lot 2319, has the standard 'Western' underframe and body sides. It has been fitted with pressed steel ends formed in corrugations, of a pattern developed by the erstwhile LNER company. No. B760563 was a 12 ton covered wagon with two large vents, one at each end, fitted with vacuum brake with the flexible pipe in the lower position and label boards bolted to the end of the wagon.

Figure 76. In many ways similar to B760563 shown on the previous plate. No. B784873 was dated 1961 and built to Lot 3398. As can be seen, the vehicle combines the plywood sides with the pressed steel ends which is not surprising, as many of these wagons were constructed for British Rail by the Pressed Steel Company, Oxford, with parts supplied by the railway factories. Note the double sprung buffers fitted to this covered van, also the brakes are of the clasp type.

The last 'ventilated van' to be illustrated in this series in **Figure 77** is one of the 12 ton double doored variety which was constructed at Wolverton in 1959, to British Rail Lot 3228. Branded 'Experimental' the end panels were of the pressed steel design and the sides were in plywood panels. The innovation on trial was the design of the doors. They were so arranged that upon pulling on the long handle, and moving this one quarter of a circle, the door opened out on to tracks and could be slid on tracks to the end of the wagon, leaving almost fifty percent of the wagon side open for access.

Figure 78. To outward appearances the vehicle illustrated on this page was another 'ventilated van' but in actual fact, this series of covered wagons (built in the years 1933–36) was made for the special purpose of conveying motor vehicles from factory to distributors or shipment. The design followed the standard Great Western Railway pattern of the period, but was different in having opening end double doors and a drop flap at each end. Overall, 350 were built to Diagram G31 on Lots 1147, 1168, 1178 and 1224.

Figure 79

Figure 79. As the short vans quickly proved their worth with the expansion of the road motor vehicle traffic, a longer vehicle was also designed which would convey two motor cars instead of only one. Built in 1930 (three years before the 'Mogo' design) the 'Asmo' was a long covered van, with a 22 foot wheelbase and also equipped with the opening facilities at each end and gas lighting for the interior. There were two separate diagrams both on the same Lot of 1059. Eighty vehicles to Diagram G26 (which had the opening doors in two halves) and 20 similar to Diagram G32, which had each half door hinged again to enable the doors to be opened in confined spaces. The 'Asmo' No. 116974 is one of the latter designs and in **Figure 80** No. 116979 shows the G26 pattern: note the variation in the end doors.

Figure 80

Figure 81

Figure 82

Figures 81 and **82** on this page give a good impression of the use of the motor car van, code name 'Asmo'. In the upper view, two Austin 10 hp saloon cars can be seen loaded into vehicle No. 116968. Cross beams and large leather straps were used as chocks to prevent any movement en route, and it is just possible to identify the gas lamp in the curve of the roof. The lower picture depicts the rear of one of the cars, with the restraining beam passing under the wings and bumpers to impinge on to the tyres. Note that the vehicle number was also carved into the wooden cross beams and burned into the leather straps.

Figure 83. A further batch of short wheel based motor car vans ('Mogo') were ordered and built in 1946–47, the design was to Diagram G43 with plywood sides in place of the upright planks of the original design. One hundred and nine vehicles were constructed on Lot 1556, and both series were versatile in that they could be used for other more general merchandise when not required for motor car traffic.

Figure 84

The other method of transporting car bodies only, was the utilisation of old carriage underframes fitted with a very light framework of steel sections and tarpaulin sides which proved capable of accommodating 8 car bodies loaded transversely. **Figure 84** illustrates one such vehicle No. 107466 which as can be seen is formed from the chassis of an early clerestory passenger carriage, complete with Dean type 6 foot 4 inch bogies. Method of loading was from the side, usually in the motor car factory at Morris Cowley, Oxford. This particular vehicle was part of a total of 111 wagons converted to this use between 1934 and 1938 on Diagrams G33 and G37 to Lots 1155, 1170, 1207, 1254 and 1317.

Figure 85 shows the vehicle with the side sheets buckled and ready for service.

Figure 85

Figure 86

Figures 86 and **87** depict the slightly different pattern of 'Bocar A' motor car body vehicle. This series, which included W85880, were again on old carriage underframes, but with 8 feet 6 inch bogies and having greater height than the previous examples — 11 feet 4½ inches from rail level, as opposed to 10 feet 5½ inches.

Figure 87

No. 11346 shown in **Figure 89** was one of the Iron goods vans which were converted for use as gunpowder vans. Photographed in 1937, this vehicle was lined throughout with timber and a pair of nailless over-boots were always kept in these vans, this was to avoid any possibility of sparks being generated whilst loading or unloading. **Figure 88** depicts the inside of one of these vehicles, which in Great Western Railway days were painted dark grey all over with white lettering except for the letters G.P.V. and the diagonal cross on the doors which were in scarlet red.

G.P.V.
IMPROVISED
GUNPOWDER VAN
G W
10 T
11346
NOTICE
NO UNAUTHORISED PERSON
IS ALLOWED
TO OPEN THESE DOORS
RETURN TO
G.W.R
NOT COMMON USER
9.2

Figure 90 shows one of the Gunpowder vans built in 1954 at Swindon for British Railways. This vehicle had a capacity of 11 tons. It was fitted with disc wheels and was painted red with black underframe. The Lot number was 2490 and the painted number was B887002.

Figure 91 shows No. B887072 which was one of the vacuum braked 11 ton capacity gunpowder vans built on Lot 2689 in 1956 at Swindon.

Figure 92 was built at Swindon in 1958 and No. B887122 was one of an order of Lot 3099, vacuum braked, with disc wheels and screw couplings. This vehicle was also fitted with double sprung buffers.

In 1927 the Great Western Railway built 12 special wooden hopper wagons for the carriage of grain. Constructed to Lot 1006, the diagram was V20. 21 feet 6 inches over headstocks the wheel base was 10 feet 6 inches. As can be seen in **Figure 93** heavy framed doors on both sides were fitted with double bolts and locks to prevent any inadvertent opening whilst loaded with bulk grain. Windows in each end were fitted with handrail and steps, also to enable staff to ascertain if the vehicle was empty or loaded. Painting was the usual Great Western Railway lead grey all over with white lettering and white roof.

Figure 94.

Figure 94 is a close-up photograph of the working gear of the grain wagon in respect of the hopper. The control wheel opened or closed the outlet at the bottom of the wagon allowing the grain to run out. Note how this gear has meant the offsetting of the brake hanger, also the movement of the door bolts was by means of a wheel and worm, rather than the more usual lever.

Figure 95 is a low angle view of the unloading system used on the 1927 grain hopper wagons and shows the opposite side of the vehicle to that in **Figure 94.** This picture illustrates the locking gear which prevented the shutter being opened other than at the unloading depot. The wheel when revolved, moved the arm transversely across the wagon so opening the bottom of the hopper, and to prevent this movement, a heavy pin would be inserted into the frame above the wheel, so restricting any movement.

Figure 95

Figure 96

Figure 96 taken at Birkenhead docks in 1927 is one of a series showing the loading of the 20 ton wooden grain wagons. This view is of the roof aperture closed and locked before being placed in position under the dock grab crane which would transfer the grain from the 'dumb' barges alongside, into the hopper wagons. The base of the grab crane can be seen spreading over the wagon on the dock track, which was just large enough to allow the hoppers to pass between its legs.

To enable the grab crane to deliver its load of grain into the rather small roof aperture of the grain wagon, large square funnel chutes were dropped into position as can be seen in **Figure 97.** This appliance was moved along from wagon to wagon as loading proceeded.

These twelve grain wagons built in 1927 were initially used specifically on the Birkenhead–Wrexham service, from barge to mill, and these seen in **Figure 98,** show the vehicles on arrival at the flour mills sidings in Wrexham. One of the roof doors is seen in the open position, and the prototype vehicle No. 42233 can be discerned on the left of the picture.

Figure 97

Figure 98

Figure 99

After only three years service as grain vans these twelve vehicles were converted in
1930 to convey cement for the Aberthan and Bristol Channel Cement Co., and their
diagram for this use was altered to V29, but at the beginning of the war in 1940 they
were again modified for the original purpose of grain carrying, but with this re-build,
the side doors were dispensed with completely. **Figure 99** illustrates No. 42236 so
converted.

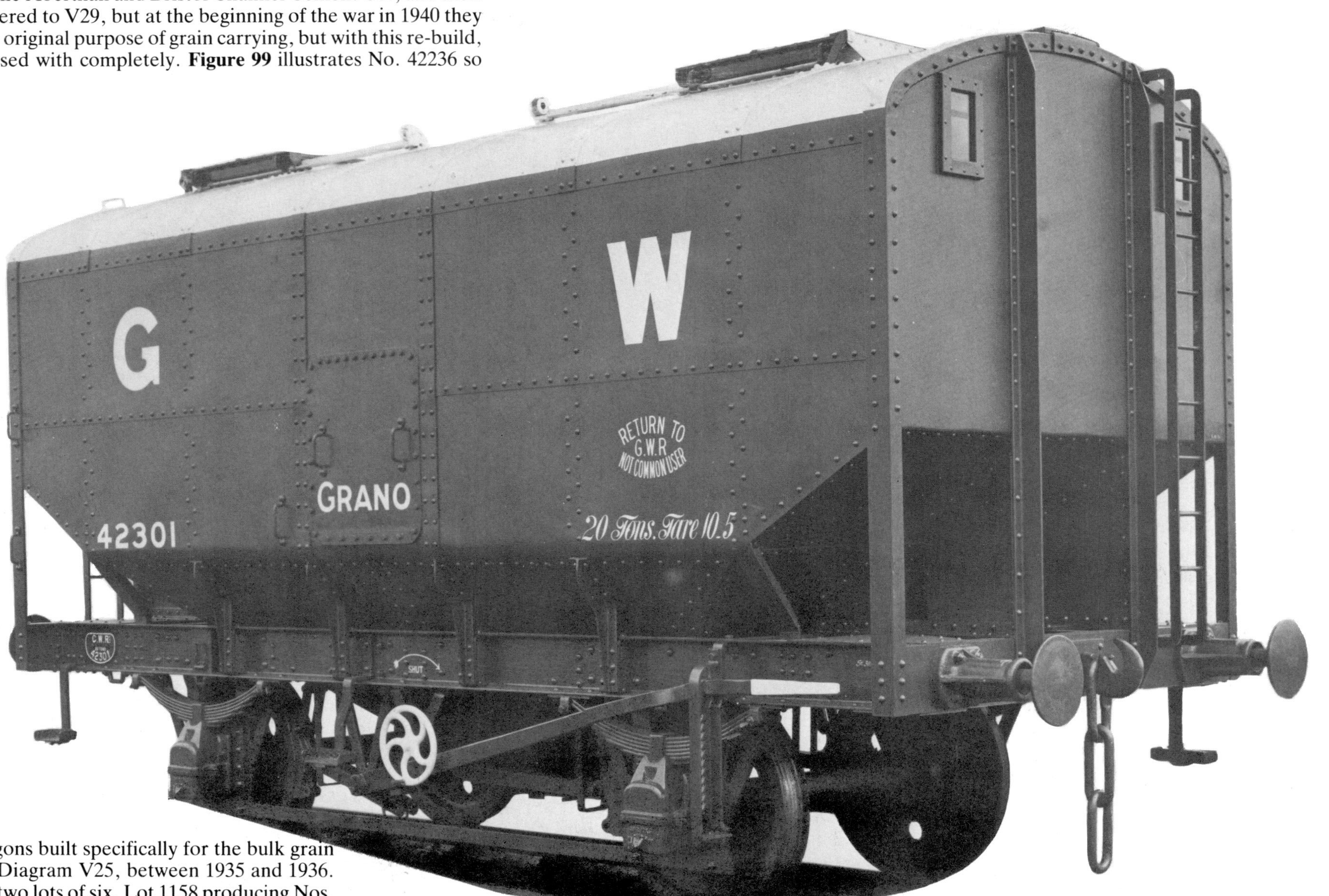

Figure 100

The next small batch of wagons built specifically for the bulk grain
traffic were constructed to Diagram V25, between 1935 and 1936.
There were twelve in all, in two lots of six. Lot 1158 producing Nos.
42301–06, Lot 1259, Nos. 42315–20. These vehicles were fabricated
in steel, and were 2 feet shorter in length than the previous wooden
design. **Figure 100** portrays the first vehicle to the new diagram, as
produced from the factory in 1935. Note that on this side, an inspection panel was fitted into the side, which would be unbolted for
access when the hopper needed cleaning or repairs to the interior.

Figure 101 shows the opposite side and end of grain hopper No. 42301 and it will be seen that there was no 'manhole panel' on this side. This was the side which had the operating gear for the bottom chute with its locking pin. Painting details were the usual Great Western lead grey all over with white lettering and roof.

Figure 102

Figure 103 shows the final picture of the all-steel 'GRANO' wagons on this page. It is of No. 42315, posed at Swindon in 1937 to make a record of the special writing which restricted the working of the vehicle. As can be seen, the service was between Avonmouth Dock and the flour mills on the Hemyock branch at Uffculme.

The roof details of the grain hopper V25 design were slightly different to those of the earlier V20. Whereas the wooden vehicles only had one roof aperture, the new pattern of all steel wagons had two openings in line with one another. **Figure 102** illustrates the fittings on top of the 'GRANO' vehicle very well, and one should note the short footboards provided at each end to enable staff to open, close and lock these sliding doors. This picture was taken in Swindon wagon yard in 1935 with an interesting background of special wagons.

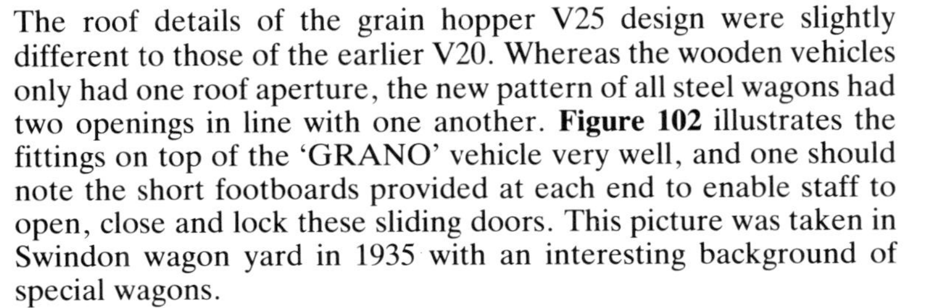

Figure 103

Another 'conversion' from the original use was the Ale wagon seen in **Figure 104.** As many as 1,250 of these vehicles were built between 1888 and 1904 for the carriage of cattle by freight train. The diagram was W1, and the vehicle was 18 feet long with a movable partition which would alter the interior from large to medium or small. These wagons were seen in hundreds all over the Great Western Railway system. However, the movement of cattle within the United Kingdom gradually moved from rail to road, and so quite a number of these cattle wagons were overhauled, cleaned and saw extended life carrying barrels of ale for Messrs. Guinness at Park Royal.

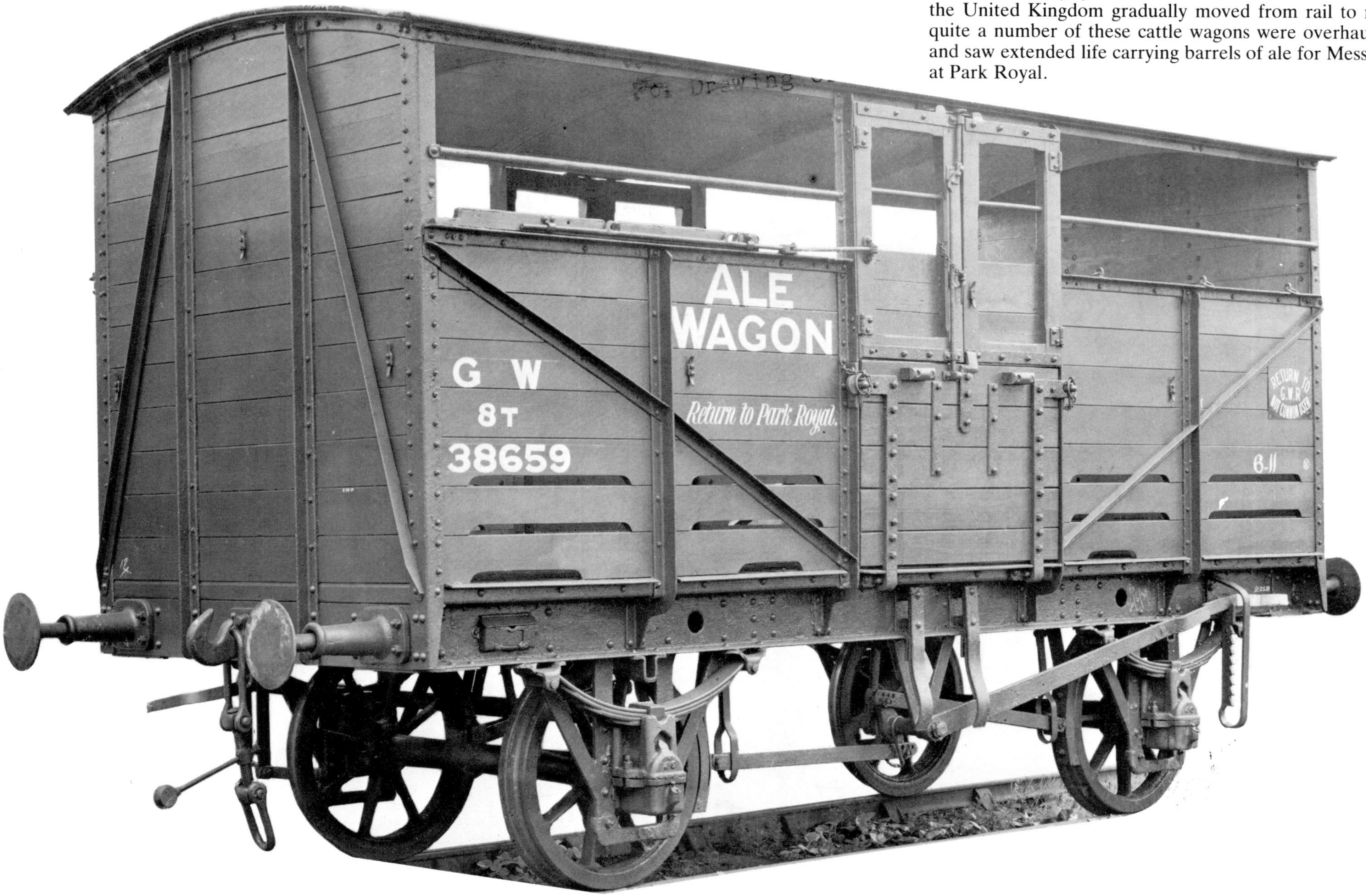

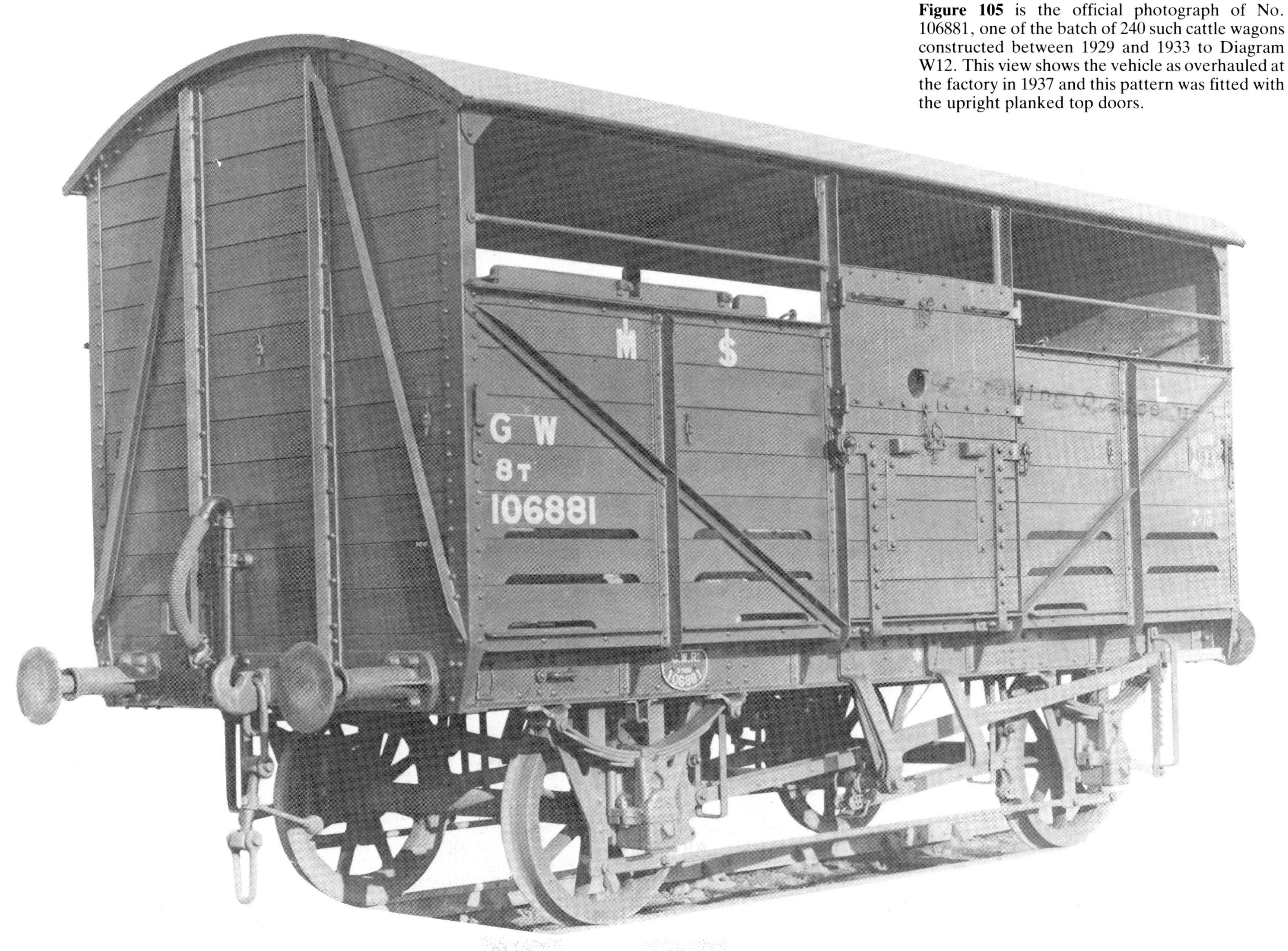

Figure 105 is the official photograph of No. 106881, one of the batch of 240 such cattle wagons constructed between 1929 and 1933 to Diagram W12. This view shows the vehicle as overhauled at the factory in 1937 and this pattern was fitted with the upright planked top doors.

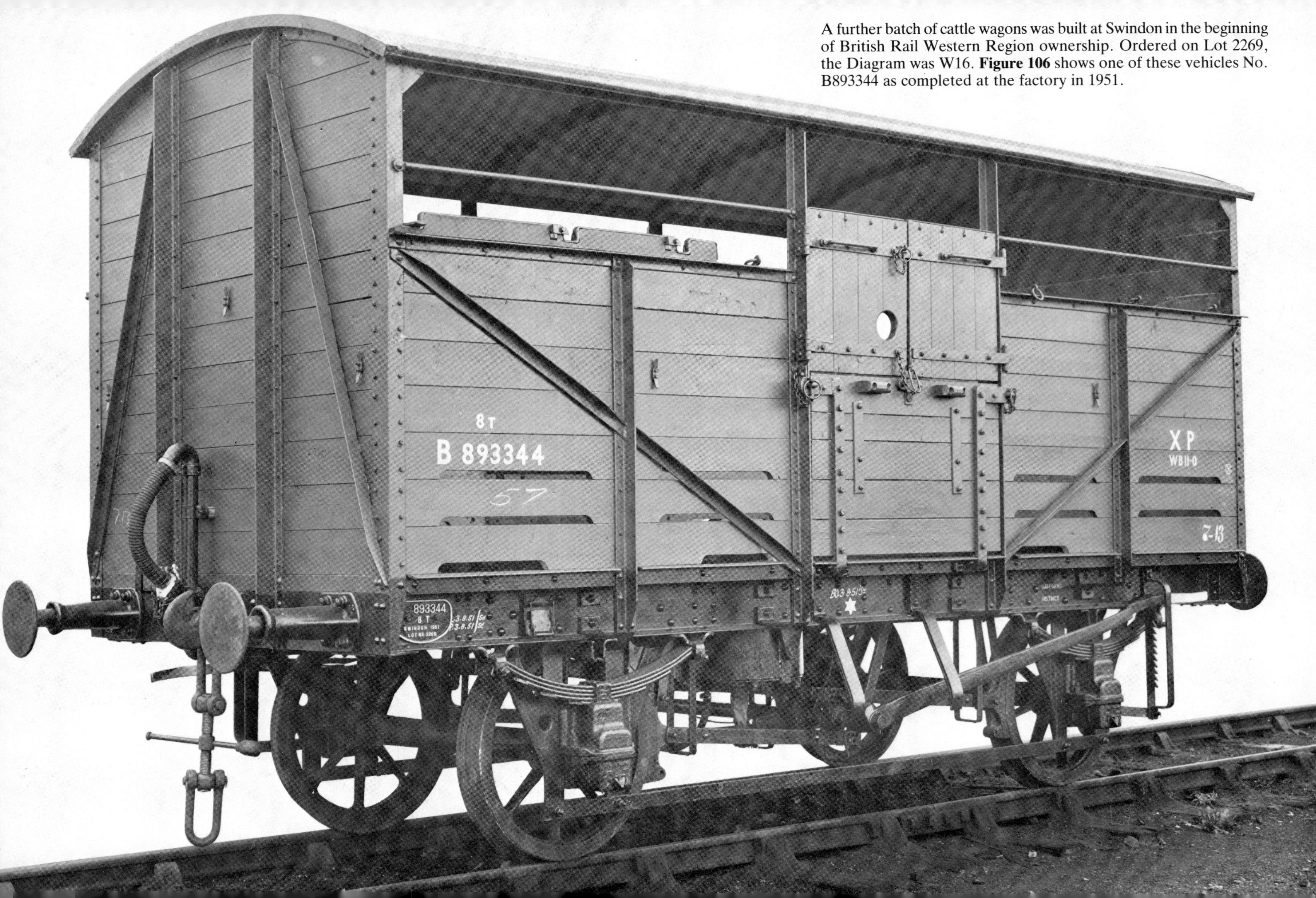

A further batch of cattle wagons was built at Swindon in the beginning of British Rail Western Region ownership. Ordered on Lot 2269, the Diagram was W16. **Figure 106** shows one of these vehicles No. B893344 as completed at the factory in 1951.

Figure 107 shows one of the last design of cattle wagons which followed the old Great Western Railway traditional designs. No. B893837 was one of a series constructed in 1952 on Lot 2325. Body colour in this instance was bauxite brown body with black underframe and with white lettering.

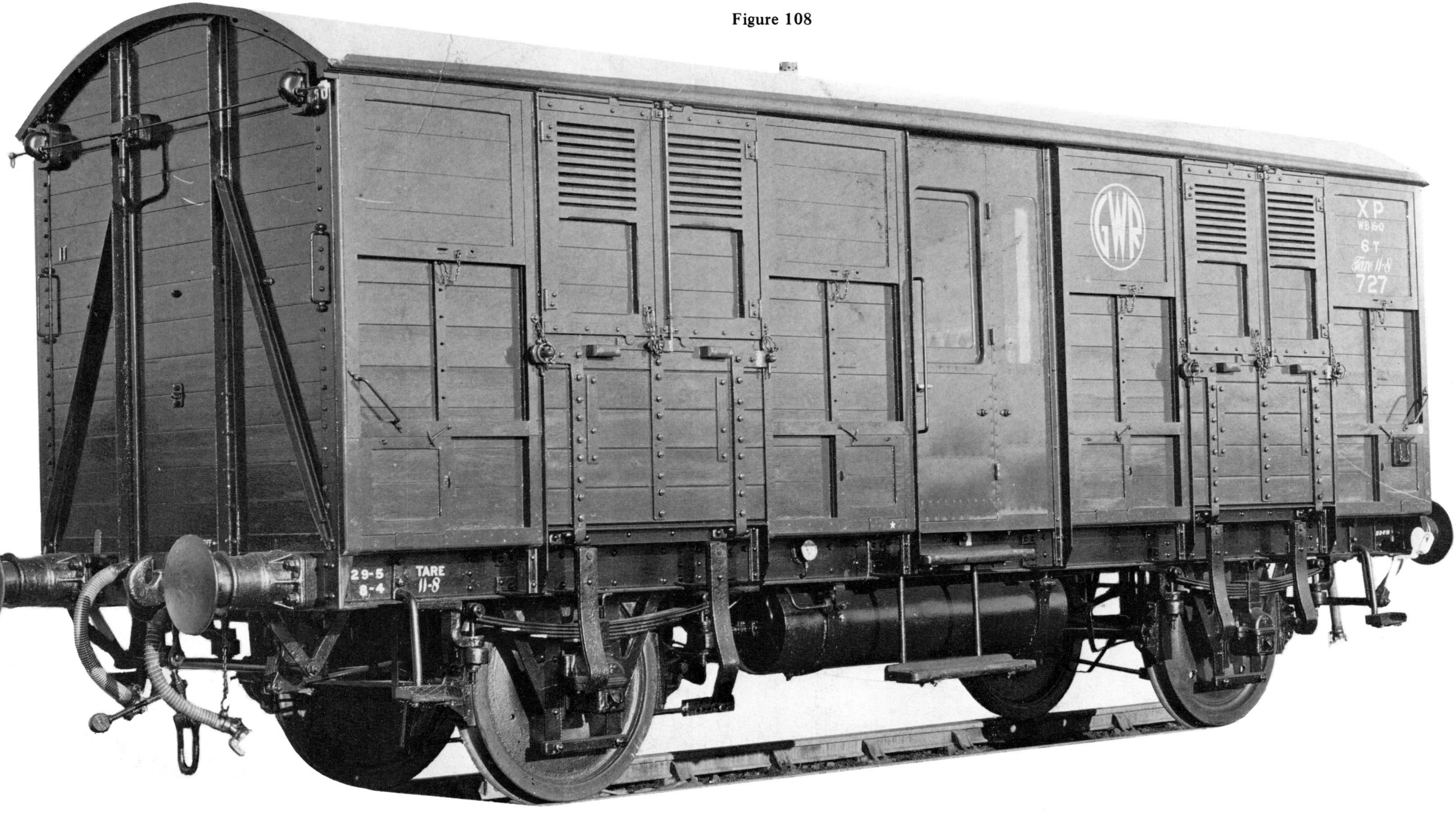

Figure 108 shows a vehicle which was used to convey cattle by passenger train. The Great Western Railway built special vehicles in the 'Brown' series, code named 'Beetle' with the added facility of a passenger compartment, similar to the horse box vehicles, but situated centrally between two loose boxes which could each house three 'beasts'. These wagons were used for carrying pedigree stock which required the watchful eye of an attendant. No. 727 was one of the batch of eleven vehicles built by the Great Western Railway in 1937 to Diagram W14 (numbers 720–730) and indeed was the last company design of cattle box to be so ordered. Lot 1605 applies. A further development of the 'Beetle C' design was constructed at Swindon for the Western Region of British Rail in 1952 and given the Diagram W17 on Lot 1728. **Figure 109** shows an example of the series, which was mounted on six wheels instead of four, but otherwise has many standard features similar to that of W14 in the previous figure.

Figure 109

Meat vans built and used by the Great Western Railway for the carriage of chilled or frozen meat were originally given the code name 'MICA'. This continued until 1939–45 war years when the old code names were replaced by 'VENT-INSUL-MEAT' and 'INSUL-MEAT'. **Figure 110** pictures one of the old 'MICA' vans built in 1889–91 to Diagram X1, after a refit in Swindon factory in 1941 and repainted in the dark grey with white letters. This was a ventilated meat van at this time as opposed to the insulated vans.

Figure 111 illustrates No. 59828 as repainted at the factory in 1941, and lettered in red paint on a white ground 'VENT-INSUL-MEAT'. This vehicle was fitted with ice boxes in the roof, and when used as a refrigerated wagon, the big ventilators at each end were closed and conversely, if used as a meat van, these apertures would be left open. These wagons were built to Diagram X7 and a hundred were built between 1921–1923 to Lot 890.

Figure 112 depicts one of the refrigerated vans built in 1929–30 to Lots 1035, 1046, and Diagram X9. This picture, taken at Swindon in 1941, shows the new painting and coding, again red letters on white, and named 'INSUL-MEAT'. Note the difference between this wagon and the example in the previous figure — this vehicle has no ventilators at either end.

The development of the container system was advanced on the Great Western Railway to a very comprehensive degree. Containers were designed and built for many types of traffic and one of these was for the conveyance of meat. Painted white with red lettering No. FX-1161 was one of the insulated types of container which could be loaded at the docks or cold store, mounted upon the container flat wagon and eventually off-loaded at its destination avoiding intermediate handling. This view, **Figure 113,** shows the container closed up and ready for the journey.

GREAT
HYGI
FX-1161
GREAT
R
39006   G
W
To be retained for G.W. Containers
39006
WHEEL BASE   9-0
20-11
8-0

Figure 114

Figure 114 shows the insulated meat container loaded on to the 'Conflat' wagon No. 39006, one of the 300 similar vehicles built on Lots 1098 and 1120, in years 1931–1933 to Diagram H6. A further 973 were also constructed to Diagram H7 between 1933–1939. Twelve more were built to H8 in 1935, 200 to H9 in the war years and 357 to Diagram H10 from 1944 into British Rail ownership.

Figure 115 illustrates one of the small all steel ventilated containers No. AX237. This pattern was painted in white with black letters. The capacity of this canister was 2½ tons and it was possible to load two similar metal boxes end to end on one long wagon.

Figure 115

Figure 116

A similar all metal ventilated container, but with double the capacity to that of the AX series, was the 'B' pattern, seen here in **Figure 116** photographed on the shop floor. This design had a capacity of 4 tons and apart from the length, was identical to the 'AX' diagram.

Figure 117 shows the standard furniture removal containers which were built to the 'K' series, being painted in the Great Western Railway milk chocolate brown with straw yellow lettering. No. K1691 is depicted here mounted on one of the horse drawn four wheel drays which were used to transport the container from the railway goods yard to the customer's residence, there to be loaded with the household furniture, returned to the goods yard, lifted on to a rail flat wagon and so on to the address and destination.

For the record, the dray was painted in Great Western Railway brown except the ends of the wheel bosses and springs which were black and cream panel along the side of the wagon with black lettering.

Figure 117

Figure 118. This photograph taken at Paddington Goods in 1935 shows 'K' container No. 1709 loaded on to a 'Conflat' wagon and with the doors open to reveal the interior. Perhaps it should be noted that these containers only had doors at one end and observe how the bottom flap covered the drawgear and allowed easy entrance.

Figure 119 shows small flat containers and were used for the packing and carriage of ceramics, tiles and similar earthenware materials which helped considerably to avoid breakages whilst in transit. North Eastern Railways six-plank open is seen at Paddington Goods depot in 1928 with the drop door lowered to show the stowage of the flat 'SL' containers.

Figure 119

G. W. R.
SL. 455
CARRY 14 TONS   TARE 6-0

G. W. R.
L. 524
CARRY 14 TONS   TARE 6-0

N

F

LOAD 14 TONS

This picture in **Figure 120** of a Great Western six-plank open No. 148250 was taken to portray the loading of the open bulk container CB2948 in 1947. This canister was in two halves, hinged at the centre, for the conveyance of sand, gravel and similar materials. On site, the container could be lifted out, the locking pins withdrawn and the load emptied by the opening of the two halves. (What I like about this picture taken at Royal Oak is the interested spectators in the tenements behind the railings.) Of the departmental wagon stock, the Permanent Way ballast vehicles were perhaps the most numerous, there being in excess of 2,500, constructed between 1896 and 1945. The simplest ballast open of them all was probably the all-steel eight-ton wagon of the P4 Diagram, built on Lots 95/147/169 and 187. **Figures 121** and **122** portray both sides of No. 60354 at Paddington Goods in February of 1928. As can be seen, there were two drop down doors on each side, with rigid centre piece and ends. This particular wagon had a brake on one side only, and was painted in the usual departmental black all-over with white lettering.

G W
60354 P WAY
Return empty to PADDINGTON GOODS
7¼ Cubic Yards
10 Tons. Tare 5-1
CONSTRUCTION
C.W P WAY
60354

Figure 123

Figure 124

The more versatile ballast wagon, P14 diagram, was built from 1911 onward and was much more practical than the P4 in that the two drop down doors on each side spanned the whole length of the vehicle. This meant that with the detachable door post in the centre lifted out, and the doors lowered, the whole side of the wagon was clear for either loading or unloading. **Figures 123** and **124** show both sides of No. 14351 in 1928.

Figure 125

Figure 125 illustrates the fixed end of one of the P4 diagram ballast wagons, the number of which can be plainly read in the photograph.

Figure 126 depicts the end of the P14 wagon No. 14351 illustrated in **Figure 123.** One or two small differences are apparent between the two designs, namely the buffers and the draw bar plate, and also the use of angle iron in the early pattern and T section in the later variety.

Figure 127

Of very similar design to the P14 diagrams was the P20 pattern of which 150 were constructed to Lot 1433 and 1500 in 1941. **Figure 127** shows No. 30480, one of this series at Swindon in 1944. Note that a step has been added at one end and the small circle containing letters CO for construction have been painted on to the wagon.

Figure 128 gives a good impression of one particular use of the P.W. ballast wagon. This was the removal of earth during the construction of a new line of track.

Figure 128

A totally different pattern of ballast wagon was built in the 1930s which made the unloading of spoil quicker and easier. This was the series of 'screw-over' side tipping wagons, with the balanced full length side doors. As the vehicle body was tipped sideways the doors being restrained by end chains swung open, so allowing the load to be discharged by the side of the track.

These two pictures, **Figures 129** and **130**, taken at Roath Dock, Cardiff in January 1931 show graphically the modus operandi. The vehicles' numbers were 100015, 100011, 100020, and 100025.

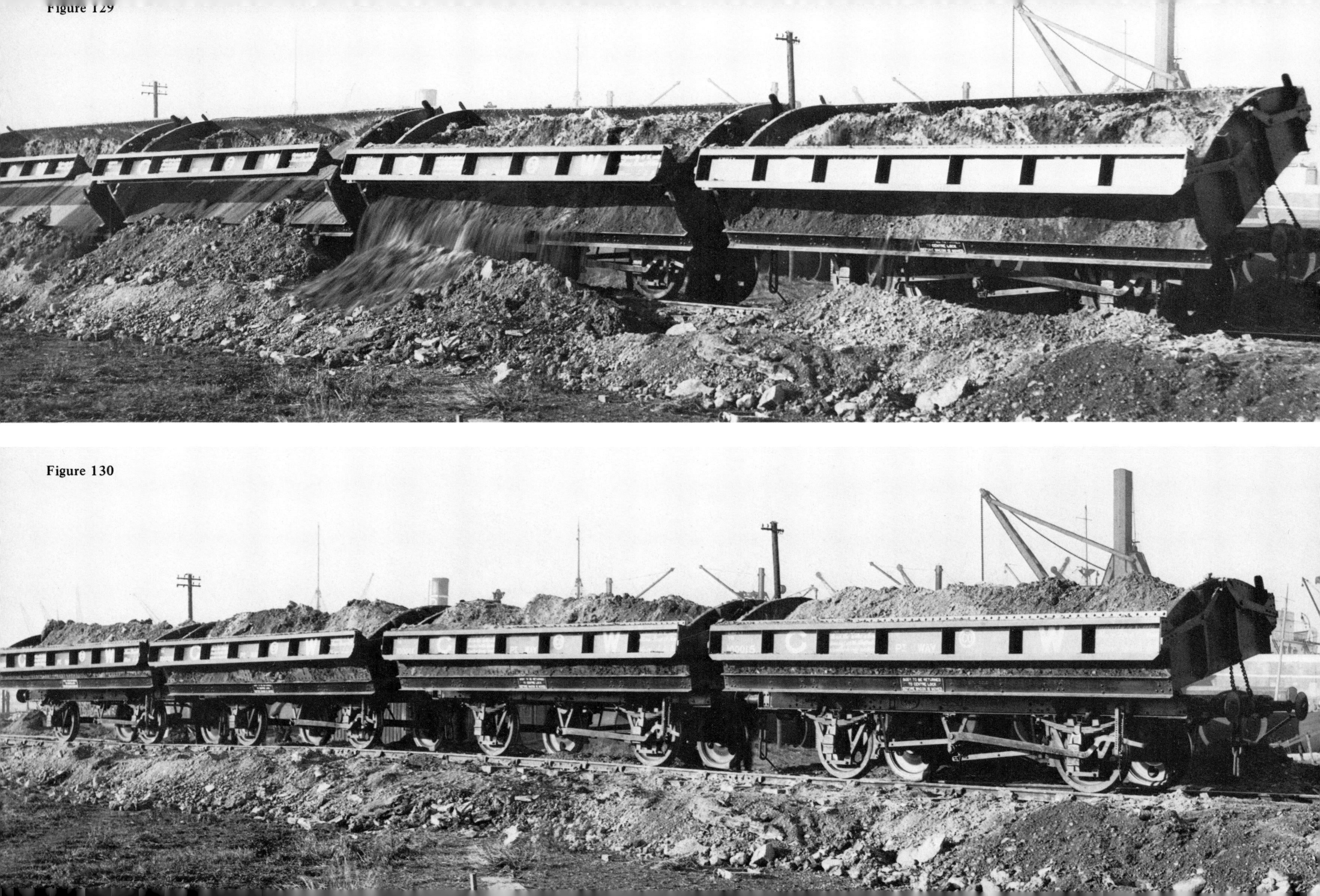

Figure 129

Figure 130

The other special ballast wagon design used by the Permanent Way Department was the hopper wagon, built entirely of steel, with an opening for unloading in the bottom of the vehicle between the wheels. In **Figure 131** No. 60005 is shown being unloaded by means of the bar just under the solebar. Pulled out, this allowed the new ballast to be emptied on to the track as the train of wagons moved slowly forward.

From 1893 onwards over 422 wagons were built to this diagram of P7. **Figure 132a** shows the train of wagons at Fenny Compton and in **Figure 132b** the Plough Brake Van No. 40373 is seen prior to lowering the plough to spread the ballast in the track.

Figure 131

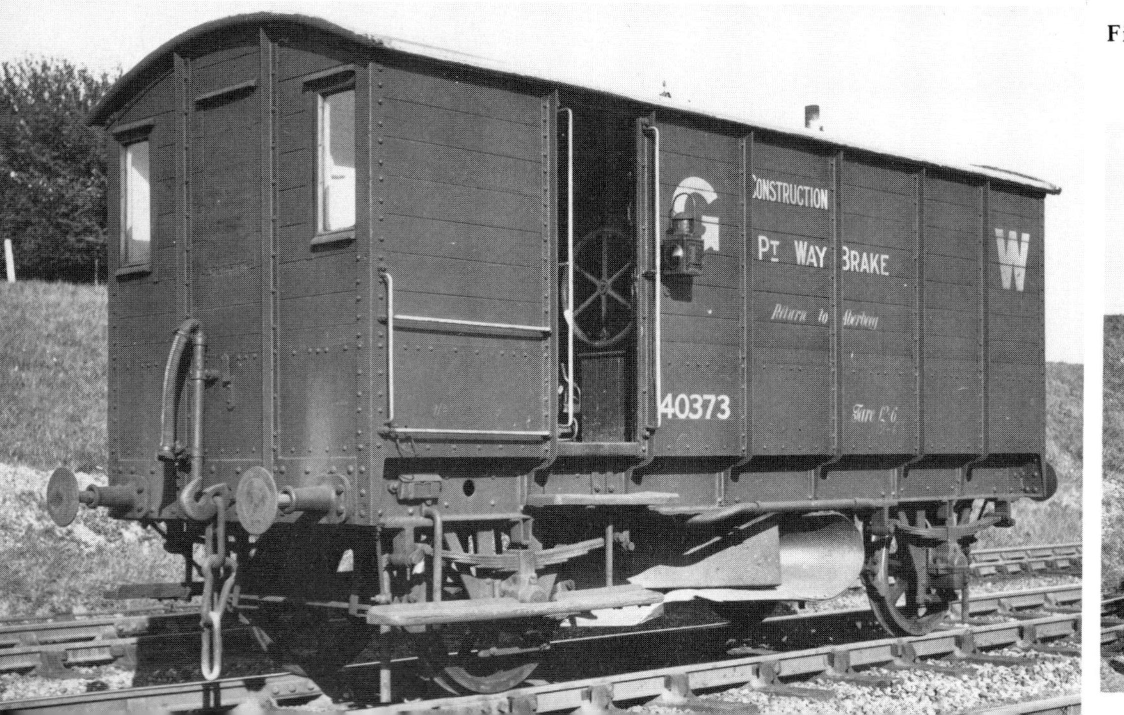

Figure 132b

Figure 132a

Flat wagons in service were used mainly for the carriage of loads which were of necessity lengthy, such as iron girders and timbers, both sawn and rough. When the physical length of the load needed more than one wagon, vehicles with central pivoted bolsters were used which allowed a certain amount of movement whilst negotiating curves. Care had to be taken when securing these loads otherwise the load could take control of the wagons instead of the vehicles managing the load. **Figure 133** taken in Swindon yard in April of 1910 shows three single bolster wagons belonging to the North Stafford Railway loaded with rolled steel channel girders where the sideways thrust of the load has derailed the dumb-buffered wagon No. 1876. The other two wagons are N.S.R. 3633 and 3868.

Figure 134 shows the same incident as that in **Figure 133,** but from the opposite side. Notice the single brake block with long lever fitted to this wagon.

Imported sawn timber in long lengths was also a load which was often carried on a pair of twin wagons, and required very careful loading to travel safely from port to destination. **Figure 135** shows an example of faulty loading at Swindon in 1903. This quantity of planks from Newport Docks is just too high for the chains to restrain them and the end view shows how the load has shifted en route.

Figure 136

This is the full side view of the shifted load (**Figure 136**) of sawn timber shown in end view in **Figure 135.** The pair of bolster wagons are Great Western Railway Nos. 70659 and 70660 and the sidings are the timber yard at Swindon factory.
Figure 137 illustrates the safe loading of rough timber on wagons Nos. 70351 and 70352 at Bridgwater in 1902. This picture was taken before the chains were applied and demonstrates a good balanced loading which would travel well.

Figure 137

Figure 138 taken at Bridgwater in 1902 is of the opposite side of wagons Nos. 70351 and 70352 seen in the previous illustration **Figure 137**. What is worth noting about the loading of the rough timber is the method of alternating the natural taper of the sawn trees. The base of one tree lying on the top end of its neighbour, thus ensuring a straight and square load.

Figure 139 shows another example of timber loading on two quite early bolster wagons. Nos. 2231 and 3637 are unusual in that although permanently coupled together, their numbers are not consecutive. Note also that the axles run in grease boxes and not the oil journals as in the picture above.

Figure 138

Figure 139

Figure 140

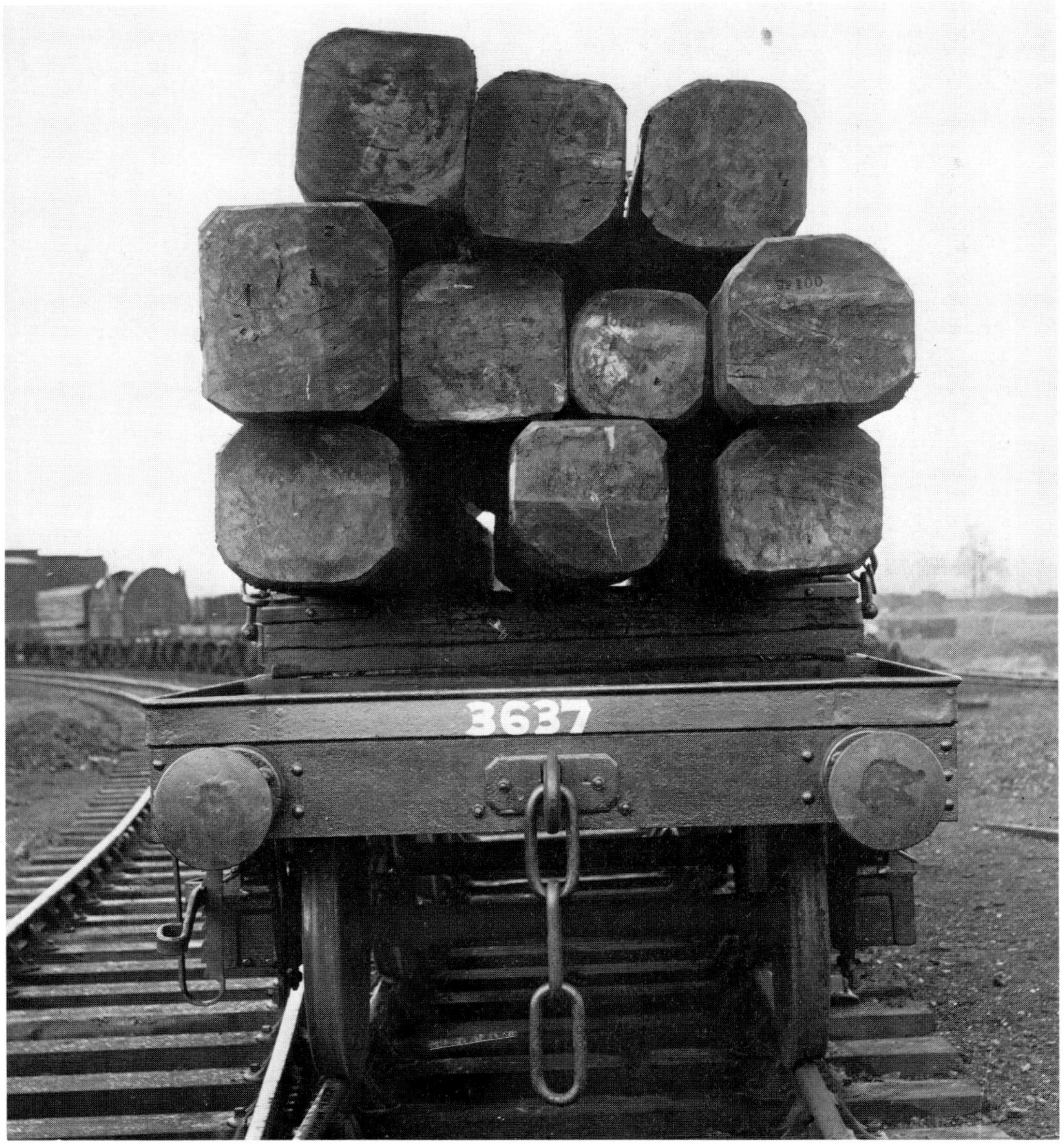

Figure 140 on this page shows wagon No. 3637 as seen in end view. It portrays clearly the loading of the baulk timbers and the number of trees carried on the two wagons.

Figure 141

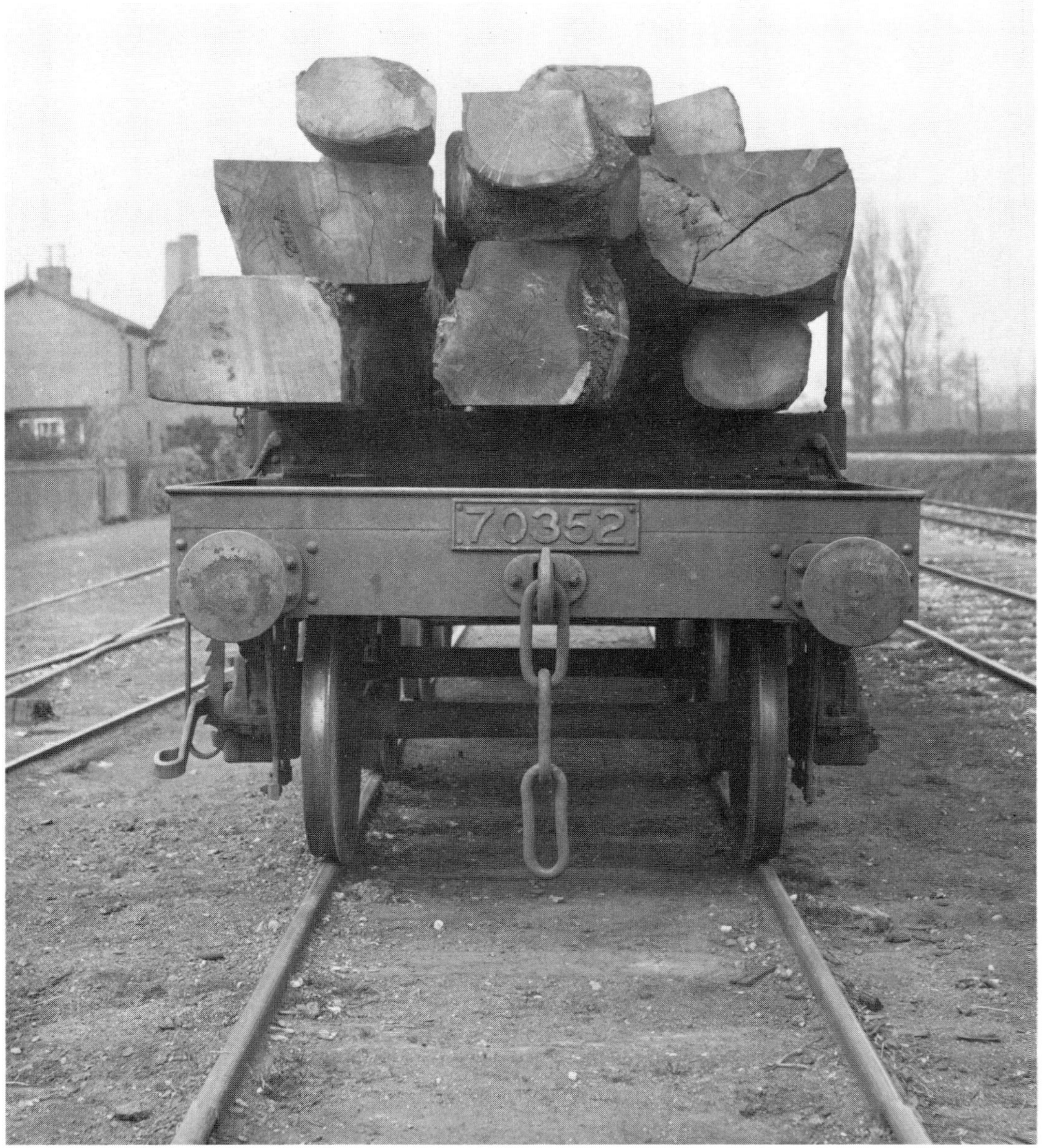

Figure 141. A similar view to **Figure 140** but of the load shown in **Figure 138.** This load was not ready to travel as the chains had not been secured and shackled up.

Figure 142. Although great care was always taken when loading any railway vehicle for transit, nevertheless, errors did occur and this figure illustrates what could happen if too many timbers were placed on a pair of bolster wagons, or perhaps the load was not secured down squarely. Wagons 8448 and 8449 photographed at Plymouth in June 1903 have obviously been taken out of service to have this shifted load corrected.

Figure 143. Taken in March of 1920, this picture portrays timber loading of very high degree. The elm sided timbers are all laid in the alternative direct so that the final load is practically square. The two small wagons (code named Mites) were numbers 48077 and 48078 and constructed to the J9 diagram.

Figure 144 is another example of good timber loading as shown in this end view of wagon No. 70101, one of a pair carrying 12 sawn trees as a full load. This picture is dated February 1902.

Figure 145

Figure 146

Figure 145 is the side view of the pair of 'MITES' Nos. 70101 and 70102, the end of one which was shown in the previous illustration. Note the style of painting and lettering at this date, 1902 and compare with the twin wagons directly below in **Figure 146**. This photograph was dated 1920 and is seen loaded with a girder destined for Penzance reconstruction.

Figure 147

Figure 148

Yet another style of painting of these close-coupled bolster wagons is illustrated in these two photographs, **Figures 147** and **148.** Taken in 1917 at Swindon, this load of old rails was en route between Wishford and Kidwelly when the load having shifted, red 'NOT TO GO' labels were attached and the wagons were pulled out of the train to be re-loaded.

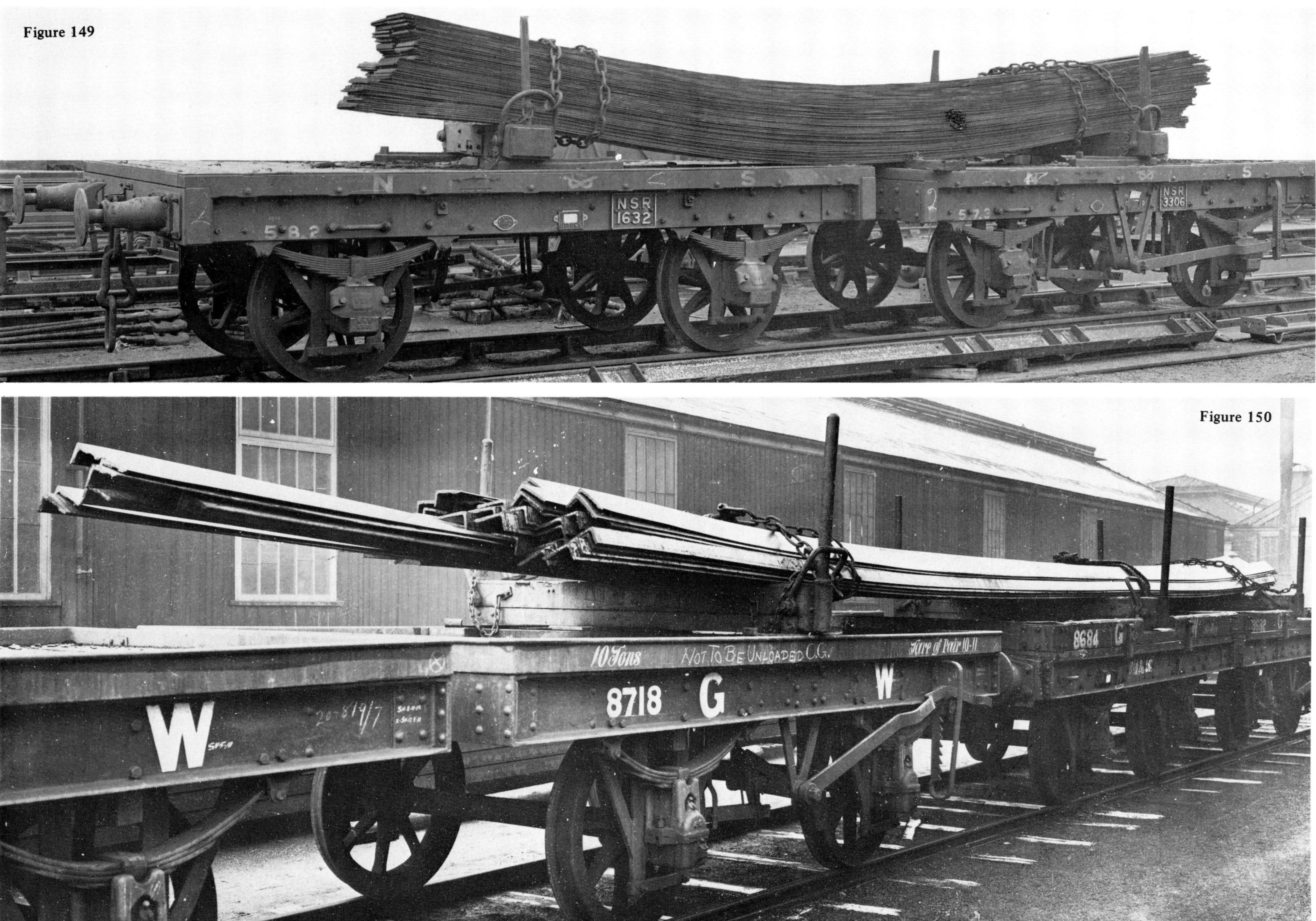

Figure 149

Figure 150

Figure 149 shows an example of faulty loading of flat iron strip. This load should have been mounted on to a single bogie bolster wagon in the first instance than on to these pair of North Stafford Railway timber wagons Nos. 1632 and 3306. Being only supported at the two ends, the load lacks sufficient rigidity to travel safely on these vehicles and has sagged down on to the centre couplings.

Figure 150 is another photograph taken at Swindon in 1910 which depicts a similar loading fault. In this instance, the angle irons are occupying two pairs of MITES, four wagons in all. This would result in a great degree of oscillation between the two pairs of wagons.

Figures 151 and **152** show respectively each side of two sets of bolster wagons loaded with H section girders which had been pulled out of their trains, because of the loads shifting. Dated 1928, these pictures were taken at Swindon Goods yard before an attempt was made to rectify the movement of the consignment.

Figure 151

Figure 152

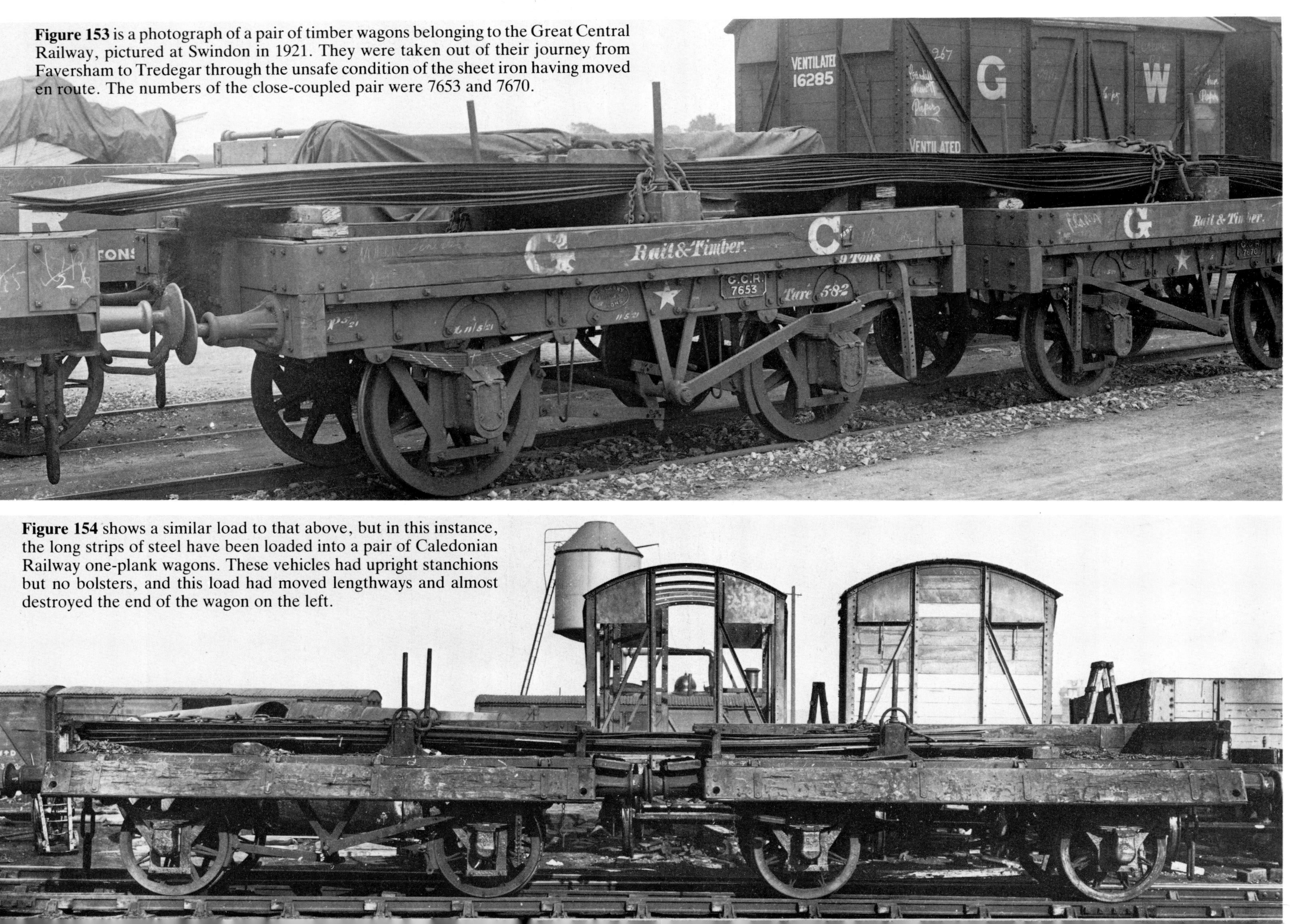

Figure 153 is a photograph of a pair of timber wagons belonging to the Great Central Railway, pictured at Swindon in 1921. They were taken out of their journey from Faversham to Tredegar through the unsafe condition of the sheet iron having moved en route. The numbers of the close-coupled pair were 7653 and 7670.

Figure 154 shows a similar load to that above, but in this instance, the long strips of steel have been loaded into a pair of Caledonian Railway one-plank wagons. These vehicles had upright stanchions but no bolsters, and this load had moved lengthways and almost destroyed the end of the wagon on the left.

Three final pictures of bolster wagons taken out of service at Swindon through shifted loads. In **Figure 155** two North Eastern bolsters carry the old rails which have slipped forward on to the check wagon of the Lancashire & Yorkshire Railway's No. 31971. **Figure 156** depicts another pair of close-coupled bolster wagons of the North Eastern Railway running with a similar vehicle belonging to the Furness Railway No. 2176.

The bottom illustration (**Figure 157**) shows two four-wheel timber wagons of the South East and Chatham Railway with a Great Western Railway 'Mite' acting as a check wagon.

Figure 156

Figure 157

This photograph, **Figure 158,** was posed at Swindon factory to demonstrate the excessive movement of long timber when mounted on short four-wheeled wagons. Note that the stanchions have had to be removed from centre and end vehicles. The date was 1911.

Used as a comparison, this is the companion picture (**Figure 159**) to that in **Figure 158** and in this instance the vehicles used are two bogie bolster wagons 'MACAW B' No. 84066 and 84060.

Figure 160

These two pictures show graphically how the Great Western Railway handled very long timbers. All of 90 feet long, these huge baulks were loaded on two bogie bolster timber wagons 'MACAW B'. It is obvious that this consignment would not traverse any severe curves such as those demonstrated in the previous pictures, but in normal traffic conditions, these short radius curves were not permitted. Notice in **Figures 160** and **161** how the upright stanchions are fitted into the outer sockets except for one bolster on each wagon.

Figure 161

As common carriers, the railways had to convey not only rough, sawn, and baulk timber, but also imported scantlings, floorboards and many varied types of wood, including pit props for use in coal mines. **Figure 162** shows a huge store of pit props at Kings Wharf, Queen Alexandra's Dock, Cardiff in 1932, and it can be seen that the method of loading this merchandise was in the upright position in standard open wagons. **Figure 163** shows hundreds of wagons loaded with cut planks, waiting to enter the timber yards at Cardiff in 1932.

Figure 162

Figure 163

Figure 164. This very unusual load forms a very special photograph. Dated 1895 it depicts one of the Broad Gauge carriage trucks No. 317 with part of a shattered Broad Gauge 2nd class carriage which was obviously involved in a serious collision. Not only is this the only picture located of a Broad Gauge carriage truck, but also the photograph reveals many internal details of the main line stock of the period.

Figure 165

Figure 166

Jumping ahead in time from the last illustration of a carriage truck of 1895, these two pictures of 1943 show conversions of old vehicles into an updated version of vehicle carrying wagons. **Figure 165** is of No. 42061 rebuilt from an early 'SERPENT' into a 'CARTRUCK' whilst **Figure 166** shows a 'CARTRUCK A' which has been remodelled from a 'SERPENT D'. The two main differences between these wagons was that one had a capacity of 10 tons whilst the other could carry 12 tons and the CARTRUCK A was of greater length in the body than its counterpart.

'CARTRUCKS' of British Rail feature in these next two pictures. Built at Swindon in 1951 No. B748011 (**Figure 167**) was the updated version of the wagons seen on the previous page. Ordered on Lot 2088, the diagram was G49 and the paintwork grey and black. Two years later in 1953, still on the same Lot 2088, the British Railways built 90 and the design is seen in B748005, in **Figure 168** (below) having several modifications from the original design.

Figure 168

Figure 169 depicts one of the series of flat wagons built at Swindon for the carriage of motor vehicles from the car factory at Morris Cowley. This picture is dated 1955 and shows the vacuum braked design No. W42179.

Figure 169

Figure 170

Figure 171

Figure 170 illustrates the 'CARFIT A' No. B748050 built at Swindon in 1954 on Lot 2265 to Diagram G52. These vehicles had the fairly high open sides, similar to the original 'SCORPION' design. **Figure 171,** the final form to be illustrated in this section, was the 'CARFIT S' which like the vehicle in **Figure 169,** was designed for traffic at Morris Cowley, Oxford. The wagon was unusual in having full drop and flaps in place of metal extensions over the buffers.

Figure 172 is of a high level view showing the deck, sides and restraining bars of the 'CARFIT' to advantage. The vehicle illustrated is No. W42179, the side view of which appears in **Figure 169.** Note the canvas straps for fastening around the wheels of the motor vehicles and the rubber covered chains which secured the chassis of the carried load.

Match trucks had two purposes in service. Originally their sole use was for accompanying mobile cranes, running coupled to these machines so that the lowered jib would be carried on these small wagons and also to act as a check-vehicle due to the overlong length of a lowered jib. Gradually many of these small vehicles found another use in traffic, acting as a check-wagon underneath any overhanging load such as timber, steel or the like. **Figure 173** shows a 10 ton capacity 'Match' truck with spoked wheels, self-contained buffers, and either side brake.

Figure 174 is one of the 'Match' truck series, built on Lot 1272 in 1937 to Diagram L23. One hundred and fifty wagons were built to this design.

Figure 173

Figure 174

Figure 175 depicts one of the smallest of 'match' trucks No. 48954 which with a wheelbase of only 9 feet was one of several which was branded 'Empty to Margam' for use with overhanging steel loads. **Figure 176** in contrast is one of the largest 'match' vehicles made at Swindon. This was No. W107107 made in 1957 especially to travel with the diesel crane No. 355.

Figure 175

Figure 176

Figure 177

Figure 178

Two wagons feature on the above page which at first glance appear to be very similar. In fact their use in traffic was very different. **Figure 177** is another example of a 'CARFIT' wagon used for the conveyance of road vehicles. No. 42169 was originally one of the 'SERPENT C' series of 1907–13 built to Lot 647 on Diagram G21, rebuilt in 1942 to the pattern seen in this photograph.

Figure 180

Figure 179

Figures 179, 180 and **181.** Three photographs taken in 1941 showing the type of wagon the 'ROLL-WAGON' on the previous page were temporarily converted to. Each wagon would carry two large crates which would contain one of the three bladed propellers used on the Wellington bomber. The three numbers seen in these pictures were 137692, 137694 and 137696.

In 1946 after the cessation of hostilities, these special wagons were converted back to their 'Roll Wagon' design.

Figure 181

Figure 178 (*above page*). No. 32038 is one of 33 similar wagons rebuilt from five-plank open wagons of Diagram O32 in 1937 to form vehicles for transporting heavy steel mill rolls. Suitable heavy duty wooden chocks were built on to the wagons to secure the load from any movement. When re-issued in this design on Lot 1275, they were given Diagram B9. In 1940 special wagons were required for the carriage of aeroplane three-bladed propellers and so these 'roll' wagons were rebuilt to design E4, for this purpose.

Figure 182 shows the arrangement of the wood chocks on the 12 ton 'ROLL WAGON' vehicles. The centre longitudinals were fixed in place and only the lateral heavy wooden blocks were adjustable, being secured by chains to the end of the wagon.

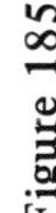

Well wagons, otherwise known as trolleys came in as many varieties as Heinz soups! These vehicles were constructed especially for transporting road carriages of all kinds by rail. On the Great Western Railway these wagons came under Diagram G and were given the telegraphic code name 'LORIOT'. On this page are three such well wagons. In **Figure 183** No. 42273 is one of the 'LORIOT L' series built to Diagram G13 on Lot 1121 in 1933.

Figure 185

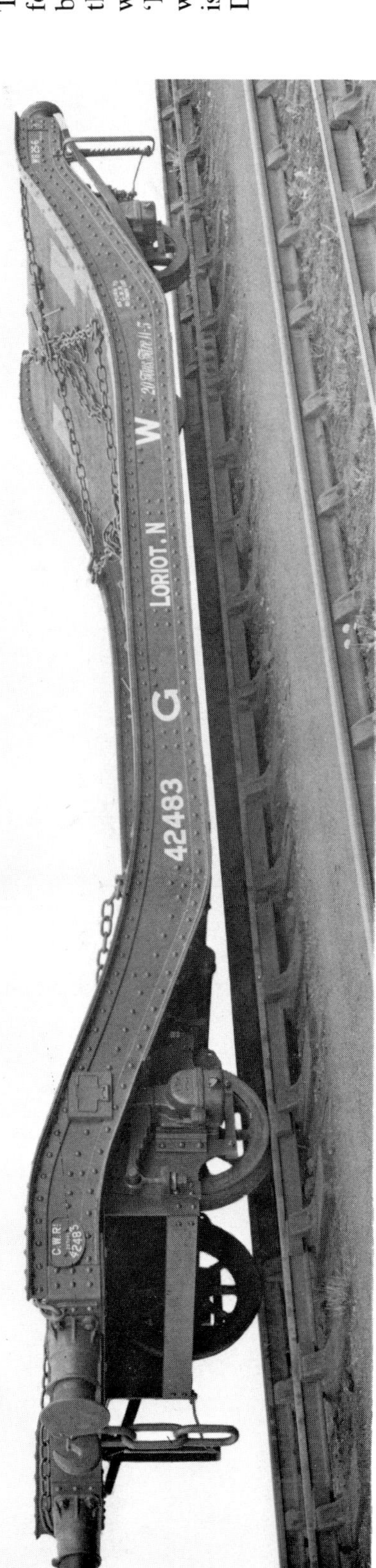

Figure 184

Figure 184 shows No. 42483, one of 35 built in the war years of 1940–44 to Diagram G40. This wagon had a capacity of 20 tons as compared with the 15 tons of the G13 design.

Figure 185 illustrates another LORIOT, this time of 25 ton capacity and coded P on Diagram G42 of 1945.

Figure 186

Figure 187

Figure 188

Figure 186 is the official Swindon photograph of No. 41989, one of only two such wagons built in 1937–39 to Diagram G39 on Lot 1274. Thirty-two feet long over headstocks, they were constructed to a similar style as the 'CROCODILE' wagons differing in that loading had to be carried out from the side as no end ramps were fitted. The writing on the end of the wagon is worthy of note.

Figure 187 shows one of the well wagons of British Rail ownership built at Swindon in 1955. Capacity of 25 tons and fitted with vacuum brakes, this vehicle was given the BR code 'LOWMAC WBB' and painted red oxide with black axleguards.

Figure 188, another 25 ton well wagon built for British Rail in 1957. This pattern was known as 'LOWMAC ES' and had the running number of B904567.

Although built specifically for the carriage of chaired sleepers, the four-wheeled well wagons seen in this old photograph were very similar in design to the previously illustrated 'LORIOTS'. These wagons had steel ends, and upright stanchions for retaining the load of sleepers. Built to Diagram T1, 12, and 13 between 1894 and 1944, 75 wagons in all were constructed and **Figure 189** depicts saddle tank No. 1249 at Hayes creosoting yard in 1912, with a train of sleeper wagons.

Figure 190

Two departmental wagons of a similar design to those early Diagram T1 seen on this page and both of British Rail design. In **Figure 190** No. DB998001 is a 'LORIOT' built for the Engineering department with removable side girders. Dated 1951 this design was given the Diagram G41. **Figures 191** and **192** show another wagon of the same series, but demonstrating pictorially just how small jibs and blocks were able to remove the buffing strut to allow for easy side loading.

Figure 191

Figure 192

Figure 193

Figure 194

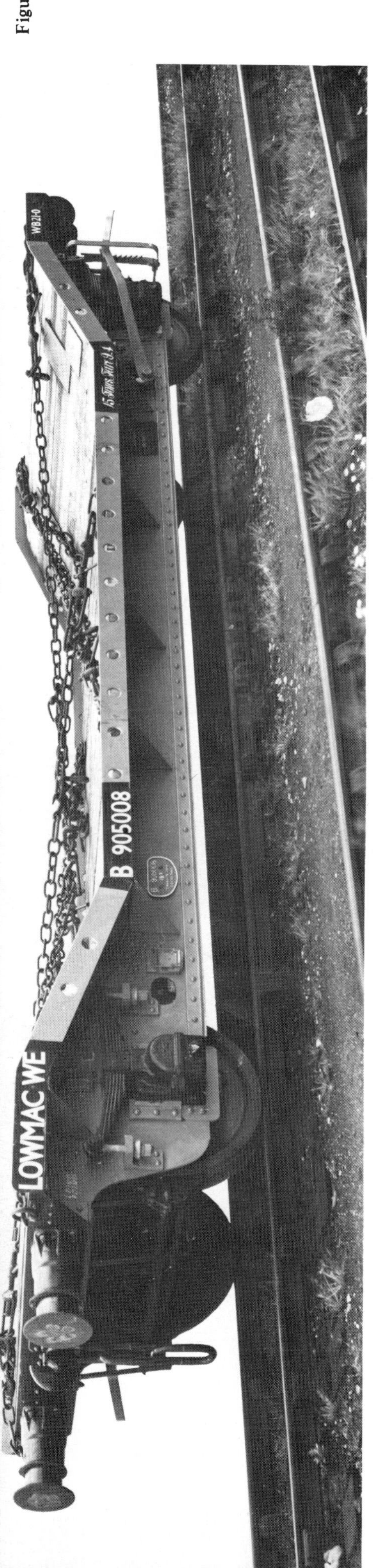

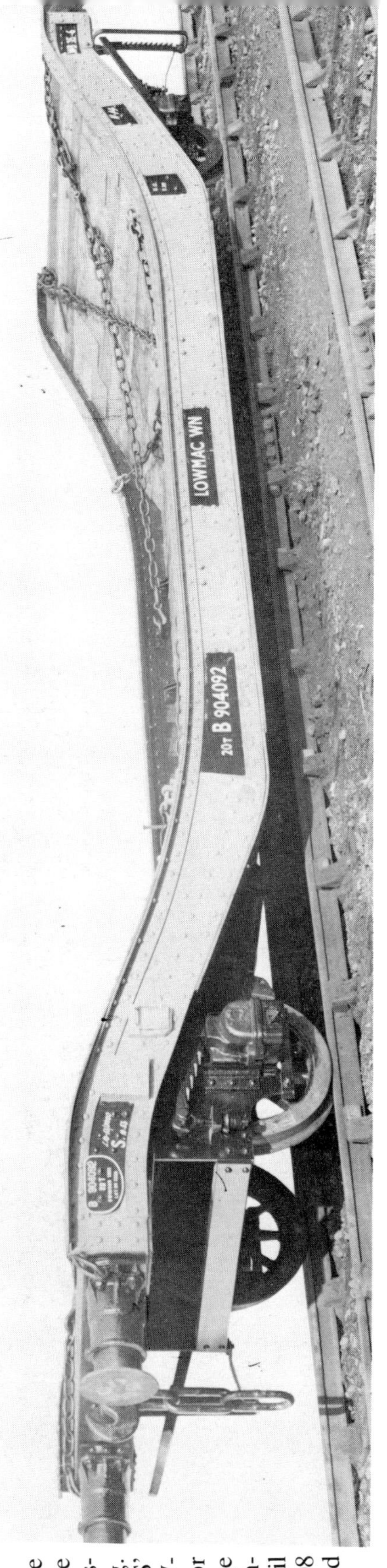

After nationalisation in 1948, when the Great Western Railway became the Western Region of British Rail, a new system of telegraph coding came into being. The well wagons from being 'LORIOTS' took on the old LNER code of 'LOWMAC' which was an abbreviation for 'Low Machinery Wagon'. On this page are three vehicles, which are of pure Swindon design, but coded into the British Rail nomenclature. **Figure 193** No. B905008 was termed 'LOWMAC WE' and dated 1949.

Figure 195

Figure 194 shows one of the 'LOWMAC WN' wagons, No. B904092 which was built at Swindon in 1953 and **Figure 195** depicts No. B904106, a vacuum braked well wagon of 1955 code named 'LOWMAC ET'.

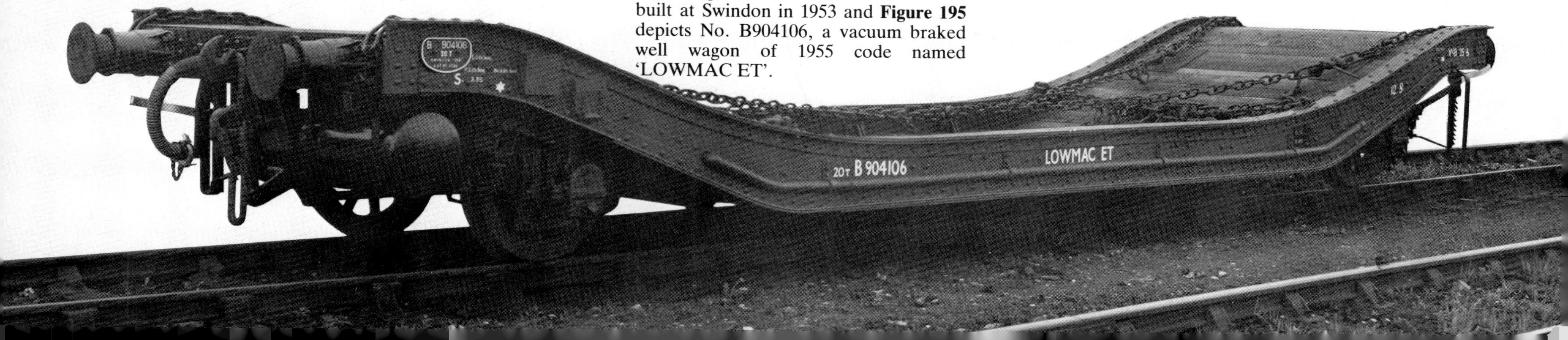

Figure 196 illustrates No. B905104, one of the 'LOWMAC WV' series which was fitted with screw couplings, vacuum brakes and roller bearings.

Figure 197, No. B904546, dated 1958, shows an example of the 'LOWMAC WP' built at Swindon in 1952.

Figure 198 shows No. B904544 code named 'LOWMAC WP' which was constructed at Swindon in 1957 for the carriage of iron moulds at Dowlais works, South Wales.

Figure 196

Figure 197

Figure 198

Figure 199

Figure 199 illustrates one of the four-wheeled well wagons built by British Rail at Swindon in 1958. Constructed on Lot 2976, this vehicle No. B904133 was of 20 ton capacity, fitted with vacuum brakes and was coded 'LOWMAC MU'.

Figure 200 shows a similar vehicle to that in **Figure 199,** but this one was of a series built on Lot 3298 in 1961, and fitted with roller bearing and the latest British Rail buffing gear. Wagon No. B904155.

Figure 201 depicts a 25 ton version of well wagon built at Swindon in 1957 on Lot 2876. This vehicle No. B904685 was painted light grey and black, and was not fitted with vacuum brakes.

Figure 200

Figure 201

Figure 202

Two vacuum braked well wagons feature on this page both built at Swindon by British Rail. No. B904103 **(Figure 202)** was constructed in 1954 to Lot 2492 and had a capacity of 20 tons and was coded 'LOWMAC WW'.

'LOWMAC SG' in **Figure 203** was a Swindon factory product of 1958 and was ordered on Lot 3101, being equipped with SKF roller bearings and the capacity being 20 tons.

Figure 203

Figure 204

Figure 205

Figure 204 is a three-quarter view of No. B904656, one of the 25 ton well wagons coded 'LOWMAC MS' and built at Swindon to Diagram BR243 on Lot 2693 in 1955.

Figure 205, No. B904721 was built by British Rail Western Region in 1958 under Lot 3198 and was a 25 ton well wagon coded 'LOWMAC WP'. This vehicle was photographed in 1960.

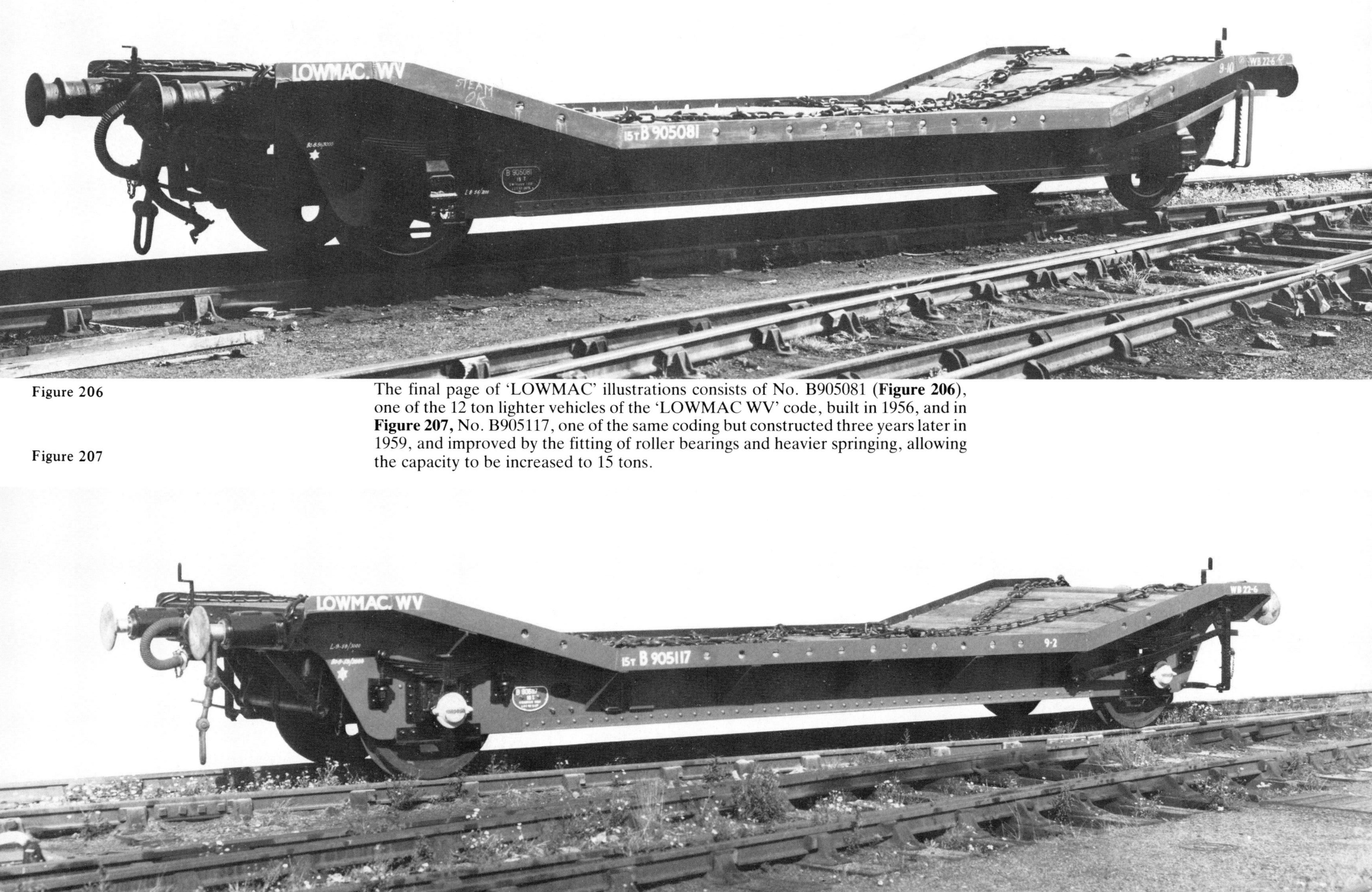

Figure 206

Figure 207

The final page of 'LOWMAC' illustrations consists of No. B905081 (**Figure 206**), one of the 12 ton lighter vehicles of the 'LOWMAC WV' code, built in 1956, and in **Figure 207,** No. B905117, one of the same coding but constructed three years later in 1959, and improved by the fitting of roller bearings and heavier springing, allowing the capacity to be increased to 15 tons.

The largest four-wheeled well or trolley wagons of the Western Region were those which loaded from the side rather than over the end. These vehicles had a very low floor with short raised ends over the wheels. **Figure 208** shows No. DB998014, one of the Engineering department's 'LORIOT' which was built in September 1959 to Lot 3201.

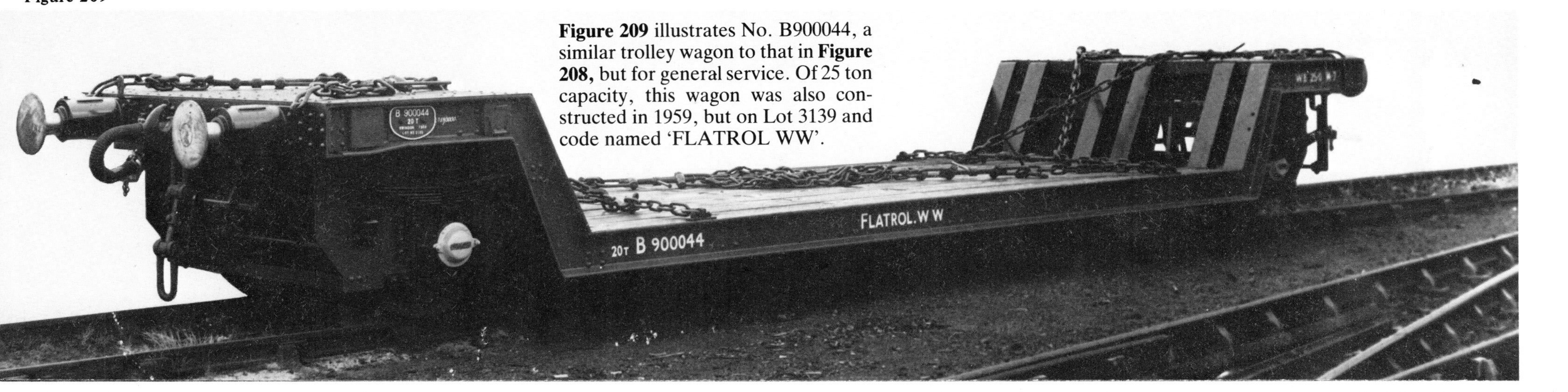

Figure 208

Figure 209

Figure 209 illustrates No. B900044, a similar trolley wagon to that in **Figure 208,** but for general service. Of 25 ton capacity, this wagon was also constructed in 1959, but on Lot 3139 and code named 'FLATROL WW'.

Figure 210

Figure 210 depicts another 'FLATROL WW' No. B900047 of Lot 2878 but exhibiting the opposite side to that of **Figure 209.** This shows the vacuum pipe fitted along the floor girder on one side only.

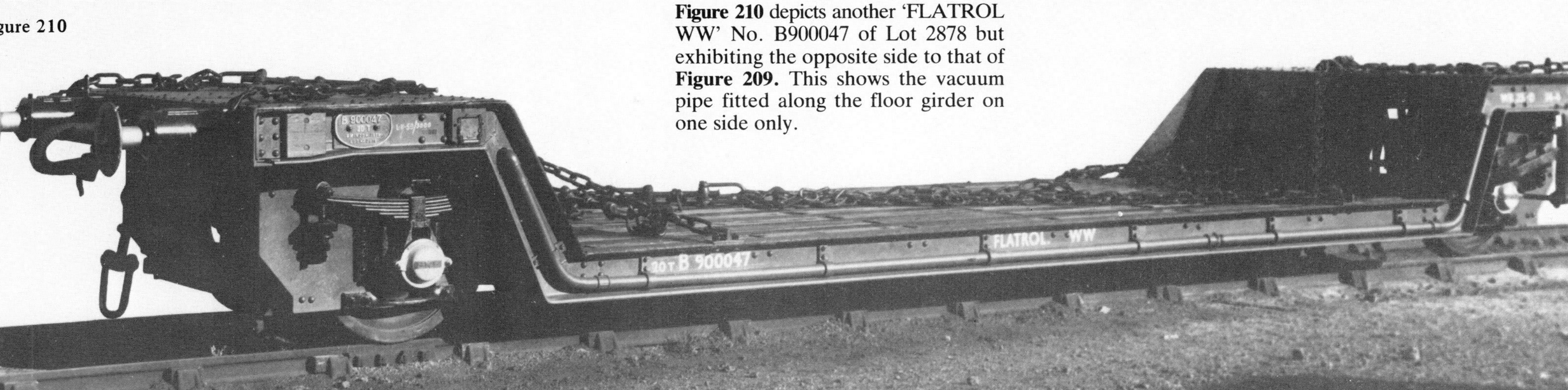

From the very up-to-date trolley wagon in **Figure 210,** the picture on this page (**Figure 211**) shows one of the early eight-wheel bogie trolleys of the Broad Gauge era (circa 1892). Although the photograph is not of first rate quality, the content is most unusual and worthy of a place in this work as it shows the damaged remains of a standard gauge carriage loaded on to a 'CROCODILE' of the 7 foot gauge, No. 11169.

Figure 212 shows the side view of 'CROCODILE' No. 11169 mentioned in the previous figure and gives a good sighting of the very close wheel base bogies, with the locomotive type wheels.

All trolley wagons of the Great Western Railway were code named 'CROCO-DILE' and suffixed with a code letter to differentiate between the various loading capacities. 'CROCODILE A' No. 41904 seen in **Figure 213** started life in 1900 as a 'CROCODILE E' on Lot 219 but was rebuilt in 1909 to the A series. It is in this condition that the photograph illustrates the vehicle loaded with a ship's propeller at Cardiff in 1920.

Figure 214

Figure 214 gives a second view of No. 41904, the 'CROCODILE A' loaded with the four bladed bronze propeller in 1920. The carrying capacity of this wagon was 15 tons loaded over the bogies, or half that figure if centrally loaded.

Another marine load is seen in **Figure 215** and is a large heavy casting shown settled on massive chocks fixed to No. 41901 'CROCODILE D'. Strangely enough, this is the rebuilt wagon which started as the 'CROCODILE' in **Figure 211**. Built as a broad gauge trolley in the 1880's, rebuilt to standard gauge and re-numbered 41901 as 'CROCODILE C' and to 'CROCODILE D' as shown in this 1912 photo.

Figure 215

Dated 1910, this picture of a motor cruiser loaded on to a trolley wagon shows the end view of No. 41948. This wagon at that time was allotted to the 'CROCODILE J' diagram and was one of only two built on Lot 600 in 1908. Both 41948–49 were later assigned 'CROCODILE E'. Note in the photograph the loading gauge spreading over two tracks and inscribed 'To Drivers and Firemen of Tunnel engines look out for Load gauges when shunting on these roads.' The site of the picture (**Figure 216**) was Acton yard.

Figure 217 (top) was taken in 1939 at Swindon yard. No. 41930 started out in 1905 as a 'CROCODILE G' with a capacity of 25 tons, but was rebuilt in 1909 to a capacity of 15 tons, and recoded 'CROCODILE C'. The illustration shows this trolley fitted with shaped chocks for transporting heavy tapered cylindrical load. **Figures 218** (centre) and **219** (bottom) show two 'CROCODILE E' vehicles loaded with exceptionally long girders, both loads using 'CONFLATS' as check wagons each end. Wagon numbers were 41958 and 41959 and the date, September 1947.

Figure 217

Figure 218

Figure 219

Figure 220 shows two more 'CROCODILE E' wagons loaded with two identical girders being moved from Horshay to Hansbridge in 1909. Nos. 41948 and 41949 are seen in service with a separating 'runner' three-plank open No. 36365. In **Figure 221**, No. 41949 is shown in closer detail and it should be noted how special boxed packings have been built up at each end to support the main weight of the girder load. These two 'CROCODILE E' wagons were originally coded 'J' to carry 50 tons but were re-assigned in 1908 to a reduced capacity of 20 tons.

Figure 221

Figures 222 and **223** both show 'CROCODILE E' No. 41949 but at different dates, and with totally diverse loadings. In the upper photograph taken in 1932, the special load shown is an exceptionally long crane jib made by Spencers of Melksham. Note the tailor made cradles and retaining chocks which are necessary for this lengthy girder. In contrast the load in the lower illustration was a horse boat or barge, loaded on edge in the trolley and retained by full length timber baulks. The date of this picture was December 1909.

Figure 222

Figure 223

Figure 224

Figure 225

Two trolley wagons assigned to the code 'CROCODILE F' feature on the above page, but containing many variations in basic design. No. 41965 was one of eight vehicles built to Lot 947 in 1925, whereas No. 41916 was first built on Diagram C4 in 1902. This was built as 'CROCODILE G' and altered to 'CROCODILE F' in 1935 to Diagram C5. Note the different main girders and other details including the carrying bogies and buffers.
Figure 224, No. 41965, photograph dated 1925 and No. 41916 photograph date was 1939, **Figure 225.**

Figure 226

Figure 226, taken outside 'A' erecting shop at Swindon works of a 'CROCODILE F' No. 41942, with a rather unusual load of two travelling crane underframes. This machinery being obviously too wide to be conveyed horizontal, has been hoisted on edge in the vertical position and secured between two long wooden beams. When in service these vehicles had a capacity of 25 tons but the interesting ancillary feature of this picture is the part view, just above the wagon number, of the mock coach body which was used on the engine No. 2021 when small locomotives were camouflaged to harmonise with trailer cars in a motor train.
Figure 227 depicts one of the heavy duty 'CROCODILE J' wagons which were capable of conveying a load of 50 tons. There were only two vehicles to this coding, Nos. 41906 and 41955. The photograph is dated 1925.

Figure 227

Figure 229

Figure 228

A pair of interesting photographs on this page illustrating the loading of a deep keeled yacht for transit by rail. The site is Kingswear in Devon where a steam crane from Newton Abbot shed is being used in place of the resident dockside crane.

In **Figure 228** the crane is hoisting the craft from a very low water berth, up over the quayside and on to the waiting 'CROCODILE' trolley wagon. **Figure 229** shows the yacht loaded onto wagon No. 41986 secured in the special cradle, roped and sheeted ready for the journey. In line astern is a sister boat loaded on to a 'CROCODILE C' wagon upon which the masts and spars of both the vessels are also carried.

Figure 230

Similar to the 'CROCODILE' but different in having a full width flat bed floor, the 'LORIOT W' and 'Y' were constructed for the conveyance of excavators, especially those with tracks which could load themselves from the side of the rail track. In **Figures 230** and **231**, a 27 ton diesel shovel is seen mounted on to wagon No. 41988, one of two such vehicles built in 1931 for this traffic. (Two others were constructed 15 years later.)

Figure 231

Figure 232

Figure 232 shows a similar design of vehicle from the London & North Eastern Railway Co. loaded with a large marine fairway buoy at Cardiff in 1934.

The next series of pictures illustrate in great detail the movement of a very large 'out of gauge' cylinder, from factory to the paper mills the final destination. **Figure 233** shows the arrival at the railway yard of the 16-wheeled road trailer which was used to transport the cylinder from its place of manufacture. Note the heap of coal on the front platform which is evidence that the haulage by road was effected by steam traction engine. The low loading trolley is seen set alongside the rail wagon which was used for the rail journey.

Figure 233

Figure 234

Figure 234 depicts the two steam breakdown cranes lifting the cylinder from the road trolley and lowering on to the 'CROCODILE H' No. 41974.

Figure 235 (right) shows the completed load, chocked, chained and sheeted ready for the final journey to Bristol.

Figure 235

Figure 236

Figure 237

Figure 238

Figure 239

Another large and weighty load carried by the Great Western Railway on special vehicles was the electricity transformer. **Figure 236** shows the transportation of one of these heavy items by road. Norman Box Ltd of Manchester were the road haulage people, and with their low loading trolley and McLaren steam traction engine, moved the transformer from the manufacturers to the railway siding.

Figure 237 depicts the arrival of the road trolley and load at the goods yard which as can be seen, cobbles allowed road vehicles to move freely across the line of tracks and so allow for the placing of the trolley directly under the traversing crane.

Figure 238 shows railway trolley wagons, in this case 'CROCO-DILE H' capable of carrying 45 tons, positioned under the steam crane which then lifts the transformer off the road low-loader, and settles the load onto the rail vehicle. **Figure 239** illustrates the final necessity, the protection of the equipment by use of wagon sheets.

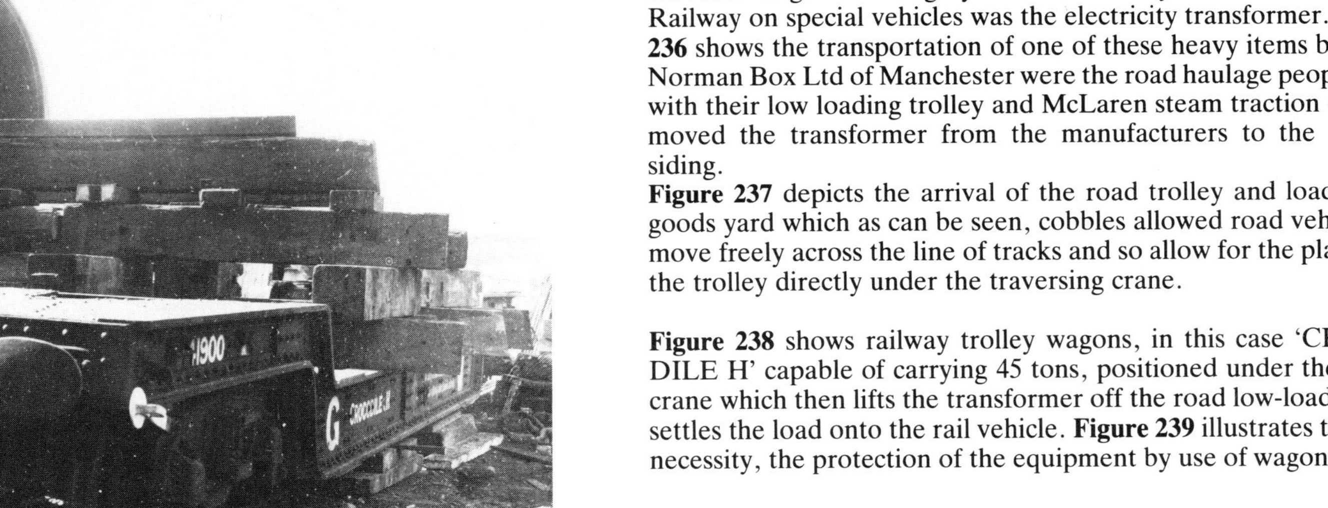

Figure 240

The next eight photographs were taken to record the loading of a heavy mill flywheel at Dowlais in 1934. **Figures 240** and **241** show the flywheel already jacked up on to chocks alongside the railway siding prior to being rolled along the guideways onto the waiting trolley. Note that the girders of the 'CROCODILE H' are also provided with chocks so that no tipping will occur when the load is transferred.

Figure 241

Figure 242

The two views on this page (**Figures 242** and **243**) illustrate the fly-wheel being rolled along the supporting beams onto the rail wagon. At this operation the wheel is at right angles to the trolley, and not only is it too wide for loading purposes, it is also too high, but at least the load is being borne by the rail vehicle. Now action has to be taken to lower the flywheel into the well, and also to skew it round at an angle to reduce the width.

Figure 243

Figure 244

Figure 245

Figures 244 and **245** show how the trolley and load were moved under the roof girders of the workshop to allow the 35 ton wheel to be skewed round and lowered into its travelling position.

Figure 246

Two final pictures (**Figures 246** and **247**) which demonstrate the load secured on to the final chocks for travelling with the correct amount of skew applied to clear the width gauge and with securing chains and shackles in place, strengthened also by two rigid angle irons bolted to the high level decking at each end.

Figure 247

'CROCODILE H' No. 41900 is seen again in this photograph (**Figure 248**) being loaded at Newport Docks in 1932 with another heavy flywheel, this one of German manufacture. Shipped from Hamburg to Newport, the load was consigned to Tredegar by rail. Note the system of empty casks acting as supports for the wagon timbers.

Figure 248

E.C.JORDAN & SON.
CONTRACTORS.
NEWPORT.
MON
E.C.JORDAN & SON.
CONTRACTORS.
NEWPORT.
MON.
RUSTON
BUCYRUS
OIL
36951
G
CROCODILE.G
W
99162

Figure 249

Figure 250

Figure 249. 'CROCODILE G' No. 36951 with a capacity of 35 tons is seen loaded with a large excavator at Wilton junction in 1933. This particular load was out of gauge and consequently would have to travel on a Sunday to avoid trains on adjoining tracks.

Figure 251

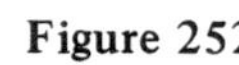

These photographs were taken in May of 1933 to record the special loading of a complete cement kiln from Ellesmere Port to Southam Road and Harbury in Warwickshire. In **Figure 250** the four vehicles can be seen on arrival at Cement sidings. One 'CROCODILE F' No. 41966 and three 'CROCODILE G' wagons. **Figure 251** records the main kiln cylinder on No. 41966 and the end view of the same wagon is shown in **Figure 252.**

Figure 252

Figure 253

Figure 254

More bulky than heavy, these Admiralty buoys were loaded in pairs on to a 15 tons capacity trolley wagon, 'CROCODILE B' No. 41922 shown in **Figures 253** and **254**. The date was April 1934 and the special load was from Chepstow to a destination at Newport Docks.

Figure 255

Figure 256 shows a whole consignment of marine buoys already loaded, checked and chained onto a whole train of trolley wagons, at the makers sidings at Chepstow. **Figure 255.** This photograph depicts the complete train of 13 vehicles, slightly out of gauge, with a brake van each end, and No. 2620 at the head en route for Newport.

Figure 256

Figure 257 illustrates another special load being lowered onto a 'CROCODILE G' wagon No. 41962. This was a ship's anchor being conveyed from Handsworth to Cardiff in 1946.

Figure 257

In 1934 (but this venue was Brentford Docks in London) the special load was a 14 ton motor cruiser. Raised out of the water at the dockside, the fixed electric crane is seen lifting and swinging the boat high over the quay and lowering on to the specially shaped chocks already fixed to the floor of No. 41948, one of the 'CROCODILE E' series,

Figures 258 and **259.** Note the wooden spacers on the hoist which prevent the slings on the vessel crushing the hull.

Figure 259

Figure 258

Figure 260

Figure 261

Figure 260 shows the boat lowered down by the bow on to the forward chock whilst the padded bags are settled on to the aft chocks. **Figure 261** records the load sitting firmly on the trolley and all that remained was to rope down securely and probably cover up with wagon sheets.

Figure 262

Two final pictures are shown in **Figures 262** and **263** to illustrate the system used to rope the cruiser down on to the 'CROCODILE E'. Note the use of ropes running in the boat's own fairleads and tightened down with the aid of screw shackles. It is also interesting to see that the rudder and pintles have been removed to avoid damage during transit.

Figure 263

Figure 264

The next series of photographs record the loading of a large 63 ton transformer onto the largest of all the Great Western freight vehicles, the 'CROCODILE L', No. 41977. This exceptional load was to start its journey at Thornhill in Yorkshire and the year was 1930. In **Figures 264** and **265** the machine is seen already supported by the long side beams which carried the load, suspended at the centre of the trolley.

Figure 265

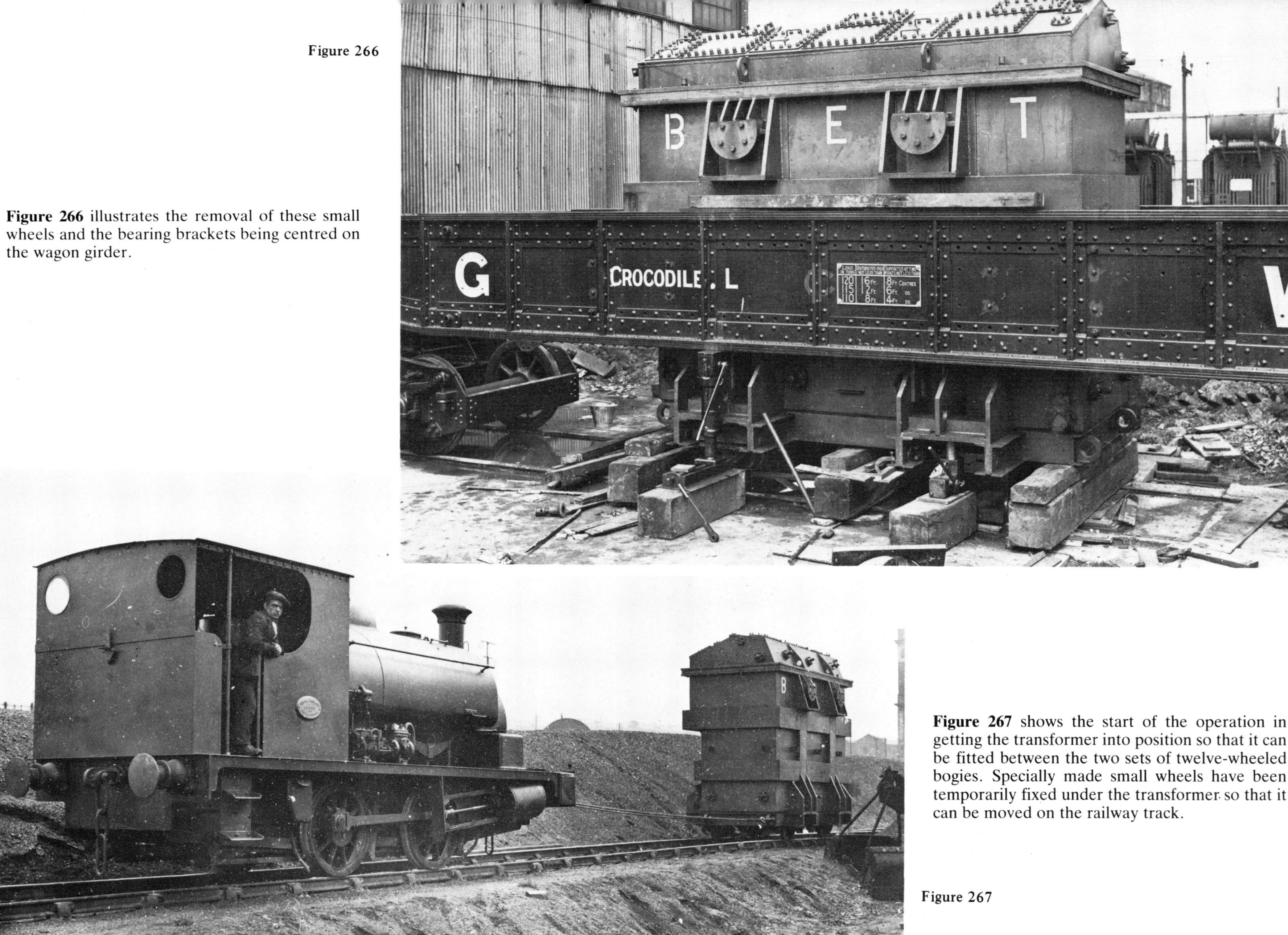

Figure 266 illustrates the removal of these small wheels and the bearing brackets being centred on the wagon girder.

Figure 266

Figure 267 shows the start of the operation in getting the transformer into position so that it can be fitted between the two sets of twelve-wheeled bogies. Specially made small wheels have been temporarily fixed under the transformer so that it can be moved on the railway track.

Figure 267

Figure 268

Figures 268 and **269** record the locating of the bogie carriages up to the carrying girders. The latter are positioned and supported by four heavy steel pins which lock the girder onto the pivoting bogie carriage.

Figure 269

Figure 270

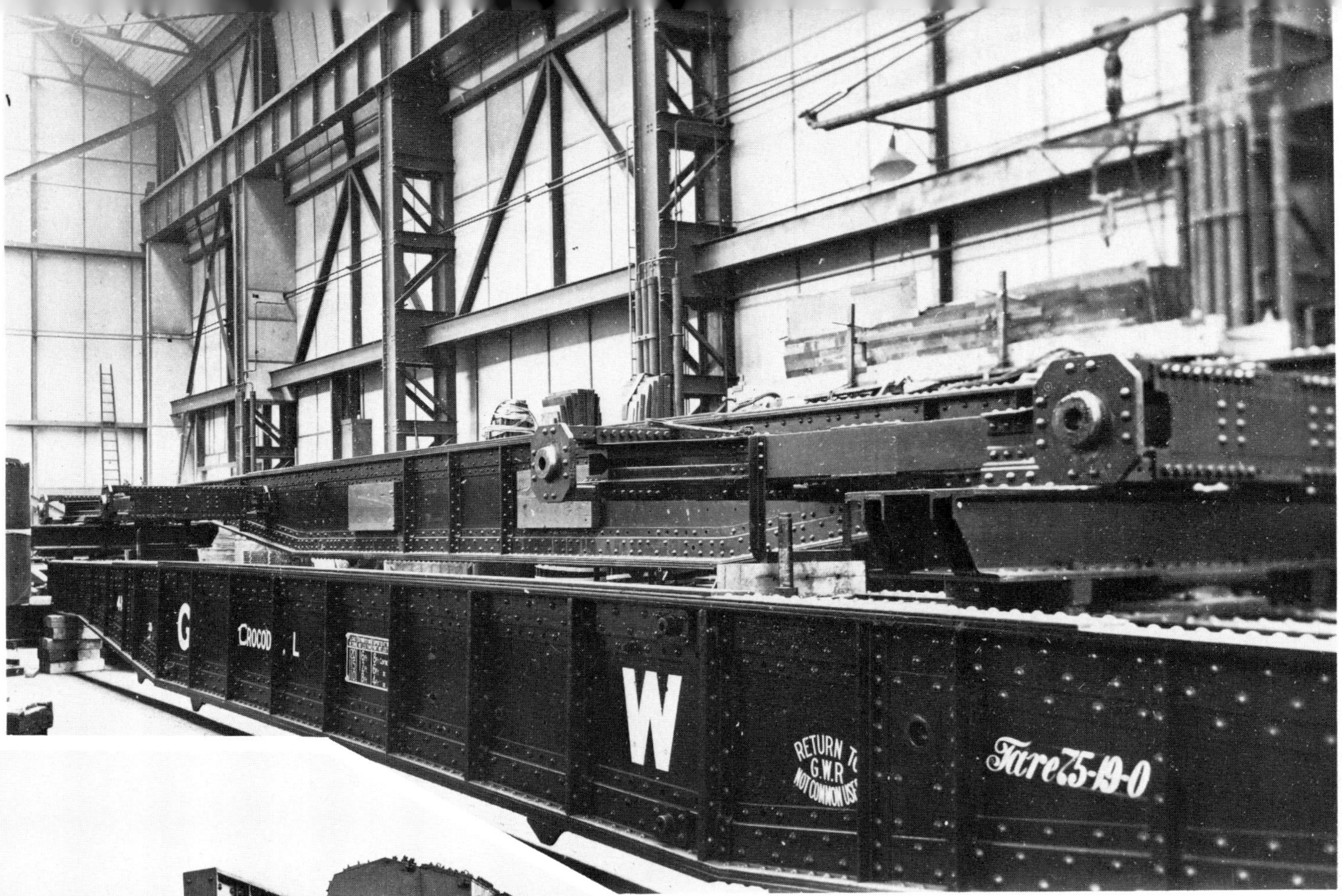

Figure 271

Figure 270 is of the straight girders of No. 41977 separated and with one lowered on to the shop floor. Note that immediately above the 'Return to G.W.R.' sign is one of the threaded supporting pins which carry the girders and in consequence, the load, **Figure 271,** is a low angle view of transformer secured into the wagon and ready for the journey.

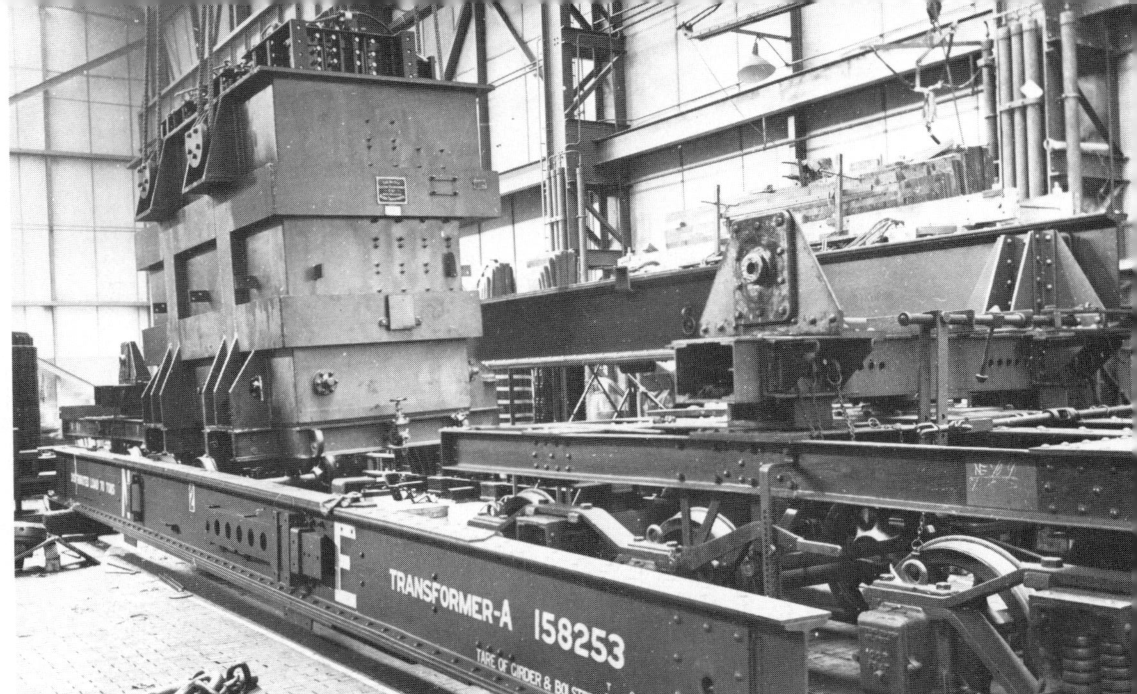

Figure 272

Figure 273

Another similar transformer, being loaded at Hayes in the same year as the previous photograph series, but in this instance the wagon being utilised is a 70 ton LNER wagon 'Transformer A'. It can be seen that the loading is very much the same as that with the Great Western Railway vehicle. One side girder taken off, the transformer dropped into centre, and finally the lowered girder being raised to support the load and pinned into place, **Figures 272** and **273.**

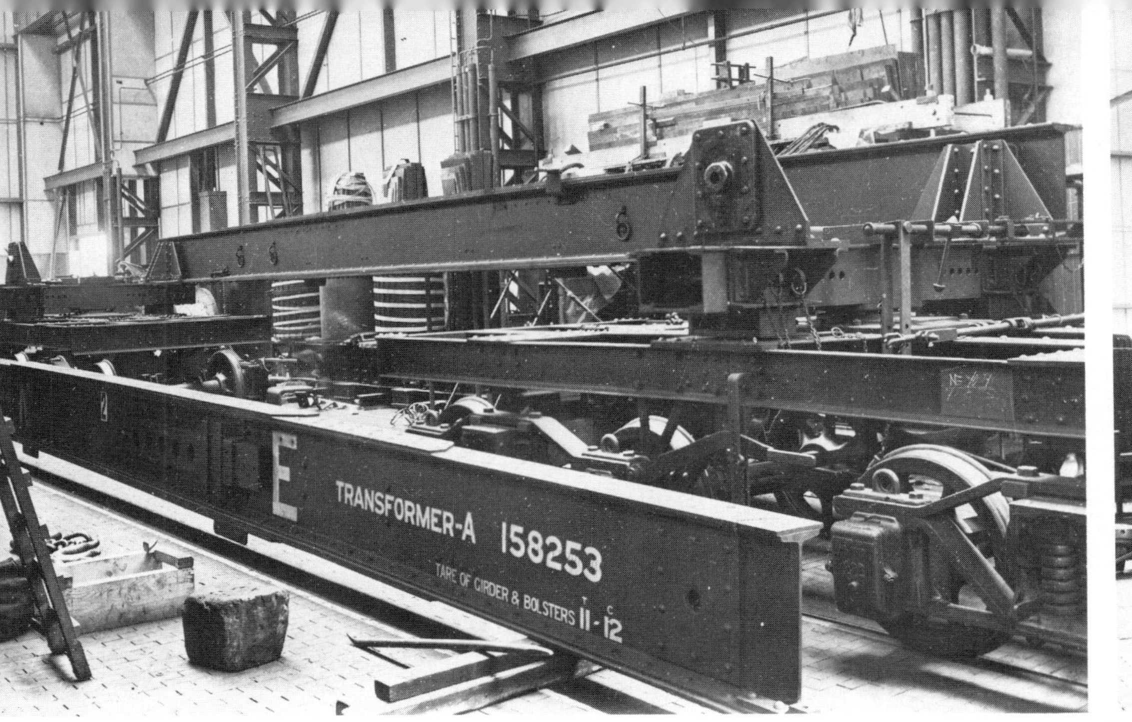

Figure 274

Figure 275

Figures 274 and **275** show two more close-up photographs which do show quite clearly how the side girders were secured into their final travelling position.

Three pictures (**Figures 276, 277 and 278**) which show the arrival of the two transformers at their destination, each on their respective trolley wagons. It is possible to compare these two big special vehicles, the LNER 16-wheel 70 ton No. 158253 with the 120 ton Great Western Railway No. 41977.

Figure 276

Figure 277

Figure 278

Figure 279

Another heavy transformer load seen on the Great Western Railway system. In this instance the 105 tons of electrical machinery was conveyed from Rugby to Buildwas in 1932 and the wagon seen in **Figures 279** and **280** was a 24-wheel trolley of the London, Midland and Scottish Railway, No. 300000.

Figure 280

Figure 281

Figure 282

In 1948 when British Rail inherited all the rolling stock from the Great Western Railway, the large trolley wagon No. 41977 was given a British Rail code name. Instead of the previous 'CROCODILE L', this vehicle became 'WELTROL WL' and is seen in **Figures 281** and **282** on duty in February of 1955 as one of a special train conveying large roller castings to Ebbw Vale steel mills.

Figure 283 shows another casting in the same consignment loaded onto an ex-LNER trolley No. 155018 code named 'WELTROL N'.

Figure 284 illustrates yet another interesting load for trolley wagons. In this instance a complete compound marine engine is being conveyed to the docks. The bedplate of the engine can be seen loaded onto 'CROCODILE E' No. 41906 with the cylinder manifold settled on the bed of No. 41961, a 'CROCODILE G'.

Figure 284

Figure 285

Figure 286

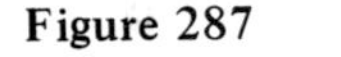

Figure 287

These pictures are a record of a special train of long bridge girders, made at Messrs. Fairfields of Chepstow, and formed into a special train to convey them to their destination. **Figure 285** is of one girder mounted on wagon No. 41932, with two 'LORIOT B' well wagons at each end as runners.

Figure 286 illustrates one end of the train with the four-wheeled well wagons acting as runners for two trolleys.

Figure 287 shows an extra long girder in the consignment loaded onto a pair of boiler wagons 'POLLEN B', and **Figure 288** depicts the locomotive No. 2465, marshalling the train prior to departure.

Figure 288

Figure 289

Figure 290

Figure 289 is the official photograph of the 40 ton trolley wagon of British Rail which was built in 1952 at Swindon on Lot 2078. The diagram was G51, the number B901003 and the code-name 'FLATROL WX'. **Figure 290** shows one of the bogie well wagons which were made during the war years for the transportation of military tanks by rail. Notice that these wagons were fitted with loading jacks under each end of the buffer beams. These jacks were screwed down during loading or unloading to save oscillation of the vehicle and straining of the springs.

Figure 291

Figure 292

Figure 293

Figure 291 depicts the first of a great tide of American built military tanks which were sent over to this country when the United States came into the War against Germany. 'CROCODILE G' No. 41944 is shown loaded with a Sherman tank at Acton in 1944.

Figure 292 shows the whole train of nine trolley wagons each with its war machine on board, and heading for the link line to the Southern Railway and eventually the Channel Ports. **Figure 293** is of a similar train but with heavier tanks all loaded on to 'WARWELL' wagons, made specially for the War Department for this purpose.

Figure 295

Three photographs in **Figures 294, 295** and **296** on this page all showing the same train of American heavy tanks en route to the embarkation harbours for the invasion of France.

Figure 296

Figure 294

The other type of bogie flat wagons built specially for the transportation of military vehicles by the War Department were known as 'RECTANKS'. **Figure 297** shows one of these wagons which were sold to the Great Western Railway between the wars. **Figure 298** depicts four of these wagons, all carrying a similar military tank from the United States.

Dating from 1900 the special rail wagon seen in **Figure 299** was known in the telegraphic code as a 'GANE'. Twenty-one were built on two lots, Nos. 258 and 290 between 1899 and 1900, numbering 40997, 40557–40596. No. 40588 seen here was one of several which were adapted to carry cast iron pipes from Chesterfield to Swindon for the Gas plant at the factory. Note the deep 12 inch solebars and the special bogies. These vehicles were normally restricted for use by the Engineering department.

Figure 300

Figure 301

The bogie bolster wagons were very versatile vehicles on any railway, being capable of conveying not only rails and timber, but also girders, road vehicles, and even large items which could be carried flat. **Figure 300** is a record of an out of gauge load which consisted of carriage underframes in crates from the Carriage and Wagons works at Gloucester in 1924. The vehicle is a 'MACAW D' No. 84365, one of the Diagram J22 series, which was built originally in 1918 for military use as J20. With the massive trussing, this series was capable of carrying 40 tons. **Figure 301** shows No. 84996, one of the 'MACAW C' wagons under Diagram J15. Only two of these vehicles were built between 1912 and 1914. The load here is factory shop overhead crane girders from Messrs. Ransomes and Rapier of Ipswich.

Figure 302

At the grouping of the railway companies in 1923, the Great Western Railway inherited a quantity of rolling stock from the South Wales companies. Most of these vehicles were in a parlous state and were carried to Swindon for either restoration or scrapping. **Figures 302** and **303** depict the ubiquitous bogie bolster wagons 'MACAW B' being pressed into service for this purpose. All the vehicles being carried were from the old Llanelly and Mynydd Mawr Railway. **Figure 304** shows a train of 'MACAW B' wagons in 1915 loaded with military limbers for the War department and destined for France.

Figure 303

Figure 304

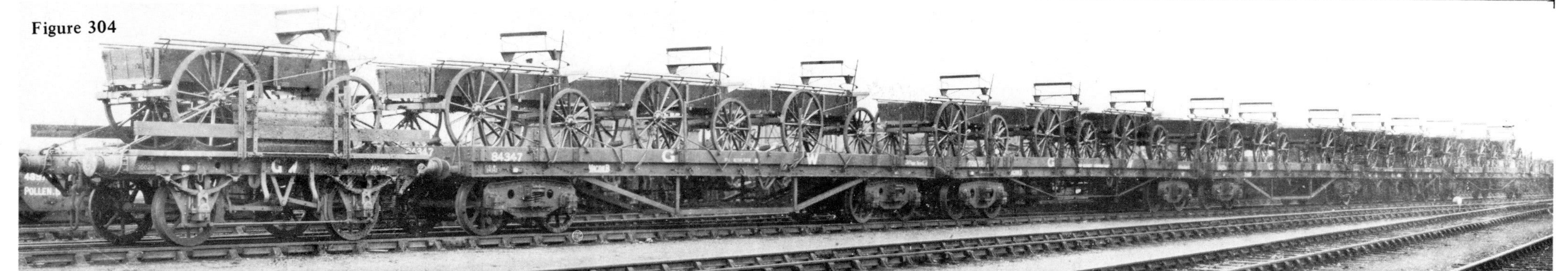

Apart from the carrying of rails, the main use for the bogie bolster wagons was for timber loading. In this picture (**Figure 305**) the loading of sawn timber is seen with the steam travelling crane at the quayside slinging the timber from the barges straight over onto the waiting 'MACAW B' No. 70815, one of the numerous J11 series built between 1904 and 1907.

Figure 306

Figure 306 taken at Hockley, Birmingham records the loading of large pieces of steelwork on to a bogie bolster wagon. The load has been brought to the goods yard on a road trailer drawn by the steam traction engine seen on the right, the stanchions were then removed from the wagon and the travelling gantry crane gradually slews the load on to the rail wagon. **Figure 307** shows wagon No. 84996 again underneath Messrs. Fairfield & Co. fixed gantry cranes at Chepstow. The load was an exceptionally long girder which necessitated the extra long 'MACAW C'. The date of the photograph was July 1938.

Figure 307

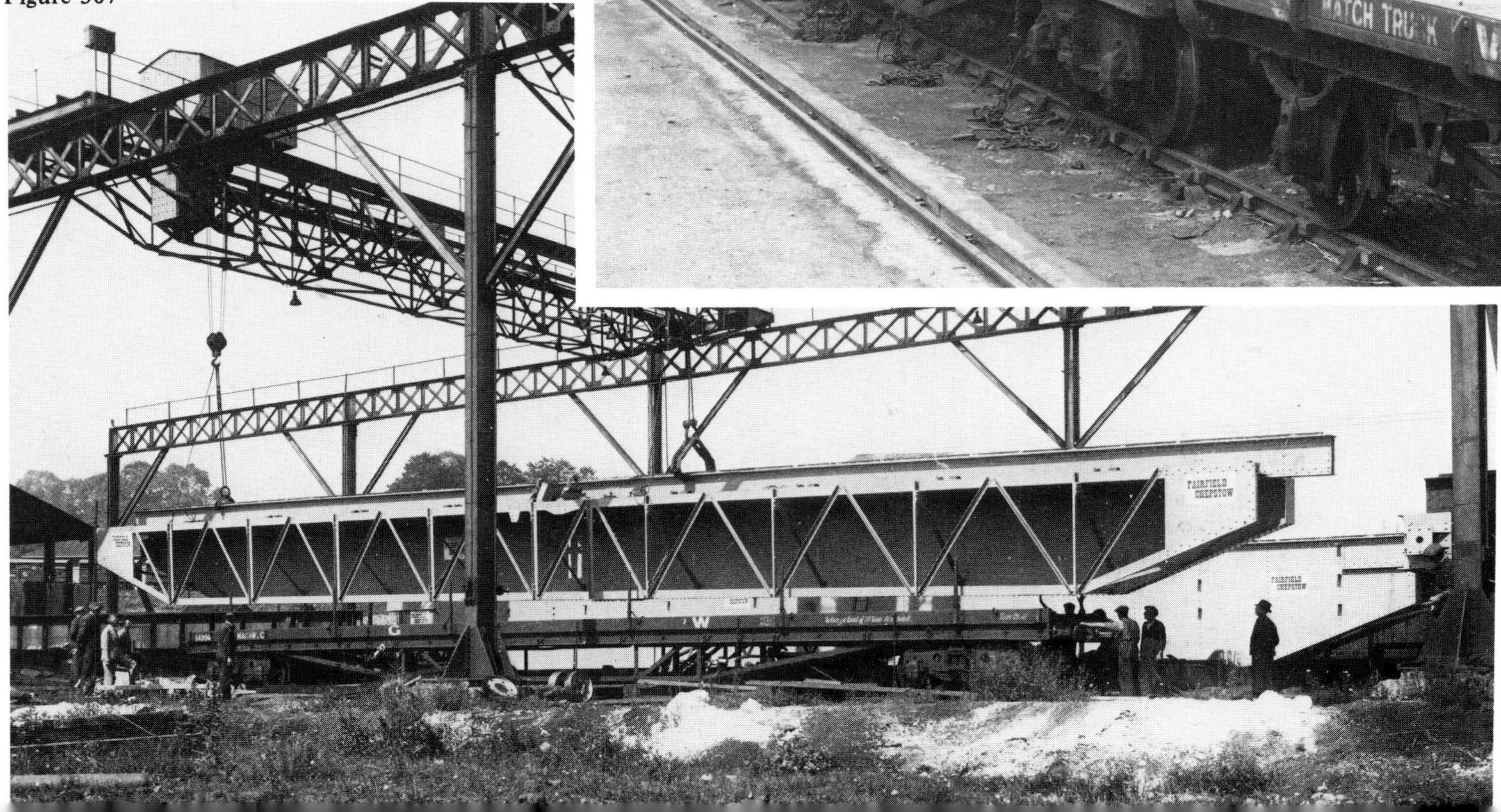

Figure 308

Figure 308 is a photograph of a 'MACAW E' No. 70736 which was built as a Diagram J24 in 1921 and then altered to convey motor car bodies in 1927, when the vehicles were re-classified to G28 Diagram. This picture was taken at the Pressed Steel Works, Oxford, in November 1927 and the load of nine car bodies can be seen stacked inside.

Figure 309 is a pictorial record of another 'MACAW E' taken in 1933 at Swindon factory with a special load of creosoting cylinders destined for the sleeper works at Hayes in Middlesex.

Figure 309

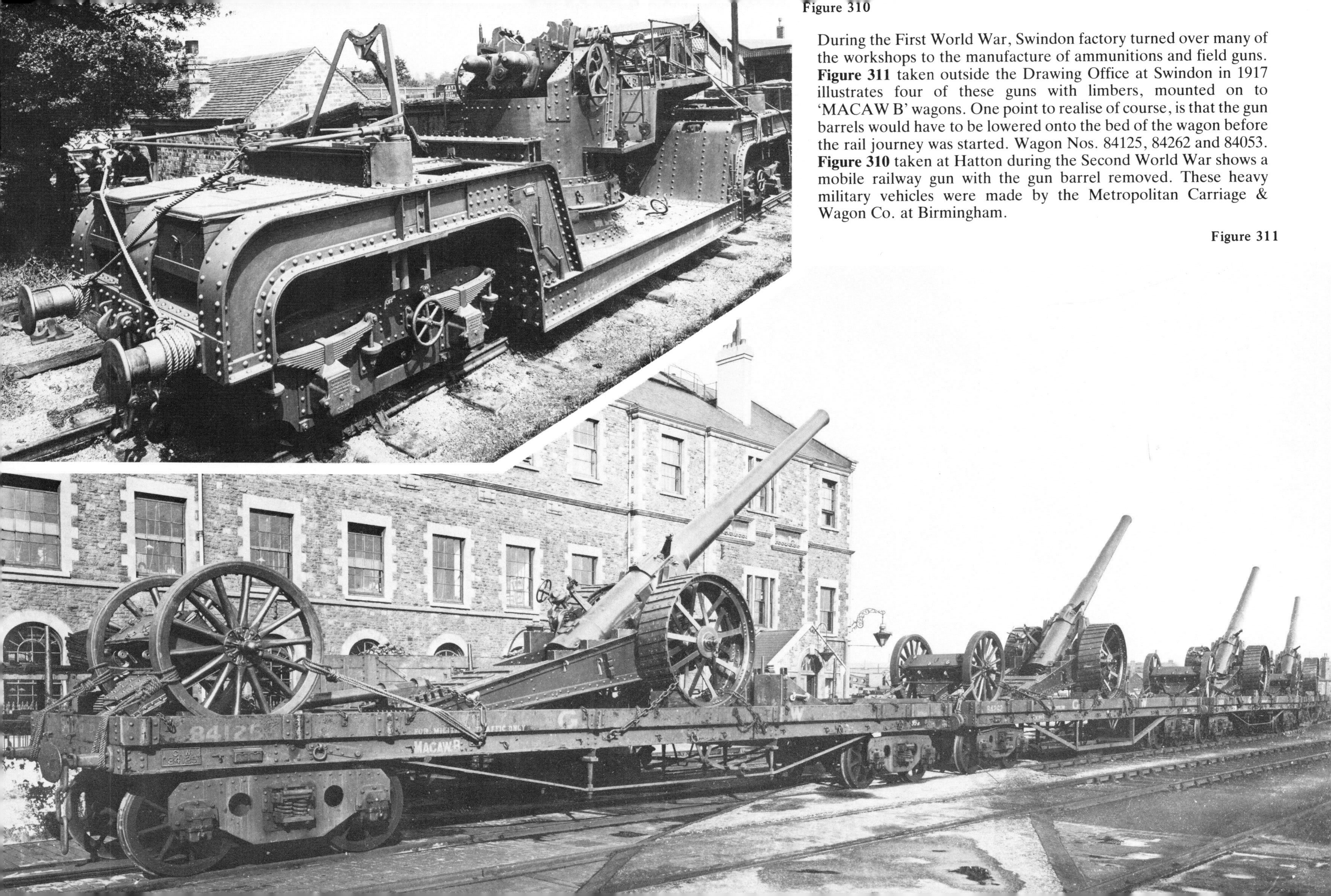

During the First World War, Swindon factory turned over many of the workshops to the manufacture of ammunitions and field guns. **Figure 311** taken outside the Drawing Office at Swindon in 1917 illustrates four of these guns with limbers, mounted on to 'MACAW B' wagons. One point to realise of course, is that the gun barrels would have to be lowered onto the bed of the wagon before the rail journey was started. Wagon Nos. 84125, 84262 and 84053. **Figure 310** taken at Hatton during the Second World War shows a mobile railway gun with the gun barrel removed. These heavy military vehicles were made by the Metropolitan Carriage & Wagon Co. at Birmingham.

Figure 311

Figure 312

On this page we illustrate a very early boiler wagon and also a modern equivalent both built at Swindon factory.
Figure 312 shows an extremely long built up girder at Swindon in the 1880s loaded on to a Broad Gauge Boiler truck. This wagon consisted of two separate trucks which could be divided at any reasonable length, carrying the load on turntables set in the centre of each wagon. Note that this 7 foot gauge wagon is fitted with grease axle boxes.
Figure 313 taken in 1961, depicts a 40 ton boiler wagon No. B907504 which in British Rail terminology was called 'GIRDER WG' but the principal and basic design is very similar to the earliest version in **Figure 312.**

Figure 313

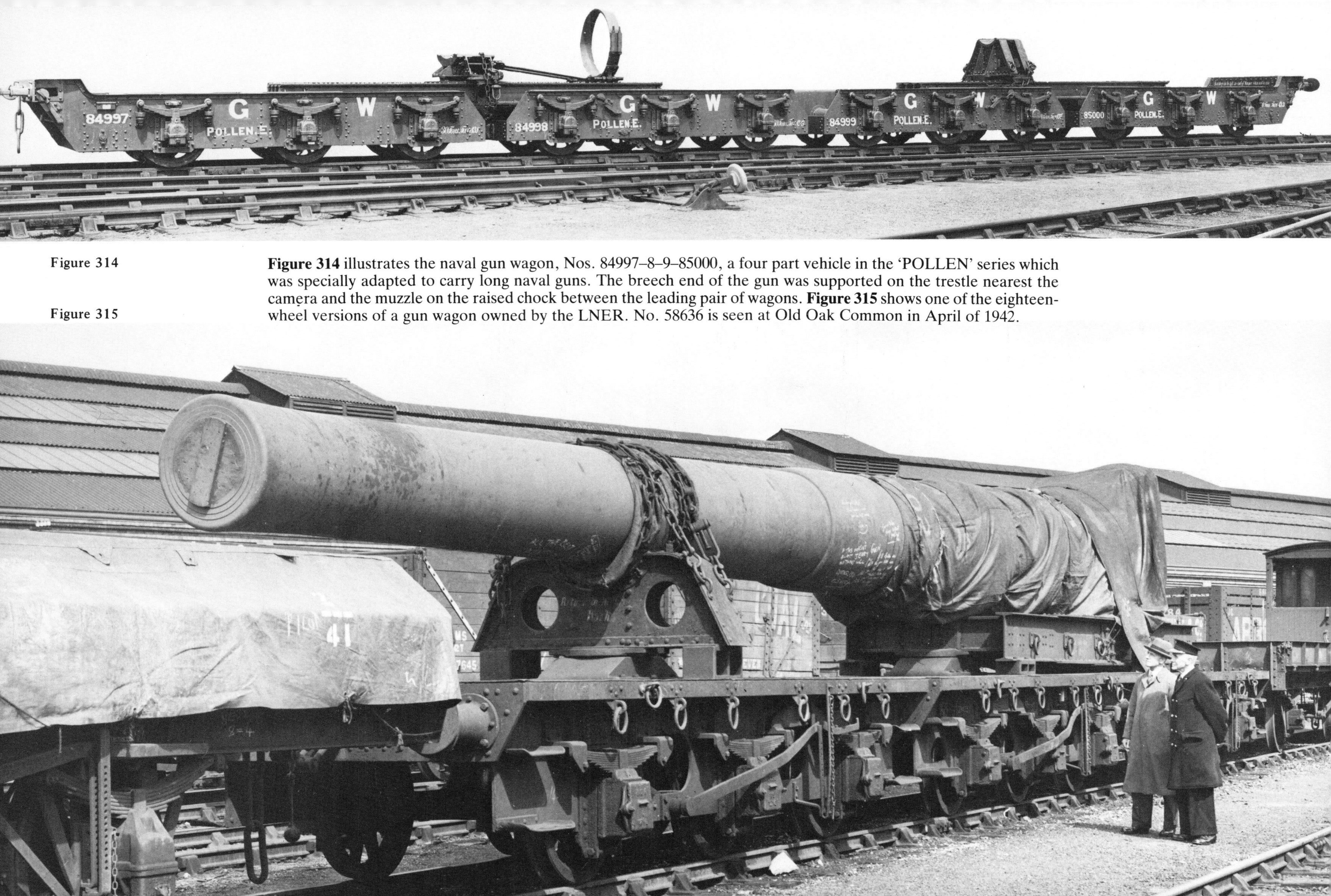

Figure 314

Figure 315

Figure 314 illustrates the naval gun wagon, Nos. 84997–8–9–85000, a four part vehicle in the 'POLLEN' series which was specially adapted to carry long naval guns. The breech end of the gun was supported on the trestle nearest the camera and the muzzle on the raised chock between the leading pair of wagons. **Figure 315** shows one of the eighteen-wheel versions of a gun wagon owned by the LNER. No. 58636 is seen at Old Oak Common in April of 1942.

This picture, **Figure 316,** illustrates two very long bridge girders made by Fairfields of Chepstow, loaded on to a Great Western Railway Boiler wagon 'POLLEN B' and a similar vehicle belonging to the LMS Railway. Date of photograph was April 1934. **Figure 317** also at Chepstow, but the date was 1932 and depicts two massive bridge girders loaded on to two four-wheeled Boiler Trucks ('POLLEN D') Nos. 32991 and 32992.

Figure 317

Figure 318

Figure 319

Figure 318 illustrates the same pair of vehicles as seen in the last photograph **(Figure 317)** but in this instance, still close-coupled together to carry the large storage tank. **Figure 319** records another lengthy bridge section being transported on wagons Nos. 48981 and 48982 ('POLLEN B'), one set of three such pairs built to Diagram A1 to Lot 379 in 1902.

Figure 320

A final page of Boiler wagons. These two photographs record the transporting of a vast lengthy girder by rail on a British Rail 'GIRDER MA' wagon Nos. 269944 and 283370. **Figure 320** is most interesting as it shows the degree of movement needed on the turntables when the vehicle is negotiating a severe curve.

Figure 321

Figure 322

The two illustrations on this page both show the loading of large heavy anvils on railway wagons. **Figure 322.** A massive anvil block is seen at Cardiff Docks, loaded on to an armour plate wagon No. 41910. This vehicle was a one-only design of 1899, capable of carrying loads of 45 tons (later 50 tons). The telegraphic coding was 'TOTEM A' and this photograph is dated 1928.

Figure 323 taken also at Roath Dock, Cardiff in 1928, depicts another huge anvil, but in this instance, loaded on to a 65 ton trolley wagon 'CROCODILE H' No. 41974.

Figure 323

Figure 324 records the movement of petrol on the Western Region. Nine four-wheeled tank wagons are shown as part of a full train at Llanwern in 1962 and in Figure 325 a line of similar tank wagons is seen alongside the petrol cranes at a large fuel depot.

Figure 324

Figure 325

Figure 326

Figure 327

Figure 326 shows another design of tank wagon running on four wheels. This is one of the specially built vehicles for I.C.I. Ltd. for conveyance of Phosgene which can give off a deadly vapour. In contrast, **Figure 327** shows a train of bogie tank vehicles carrying petrol for the Gulf concern and is seen in 1968 passing Caerlean.

Figures 328 (on this page), **329** and **330** (below). The problem of vegetation growing in the permanent way has always created a nuisance, and to make eradication of these weeds easier than the pick and shovel method, several schemes have been tried. These next pictures show how the Great Western Railway gave an extensive trial to an elaborate system of weed-killing. As can be seen, old locomotive tenders were pressed into service as storage tanks of the chemical, and the front end of one was fitted with sprays and controls. Two brake vans for staff and No. 5727 Pannier Tank, and the unit could deal with many miles of track at one loading.

Figure 329

Figure 330

Figure 331

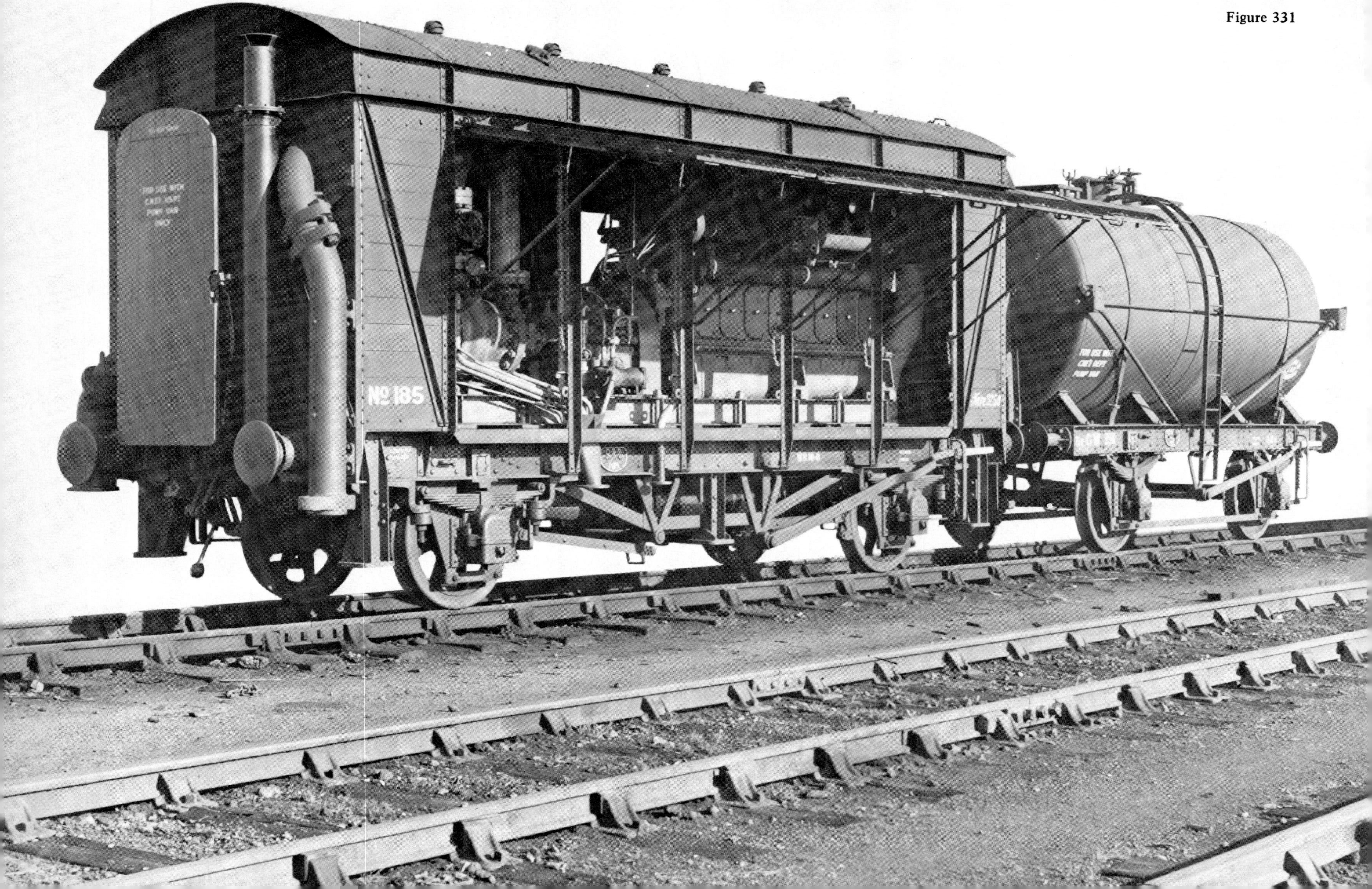

Figure 331 (above) is a record of the special pump van which was constructed for use in the docks in South Wales. No. 185 is seen in this view with the door sides fully open, exposing the big diesel engine and the compressor pump. This unit was usually coupled to Tank wagon No. 191 which supplied the fuel oil to keep this powerful mobile pump in action.

Figure 332. Many freight vehicles of the Great Western Railway were adapted and converted to other duties than their original normal routine and some wagons were selected for one particular service. No. 201 seen here is one of Lot 510, Diagram V9 which was painted into the brown series and used for transporting locomotive parts from Swindon to outlying steam sheds in 1948.

Figure 332

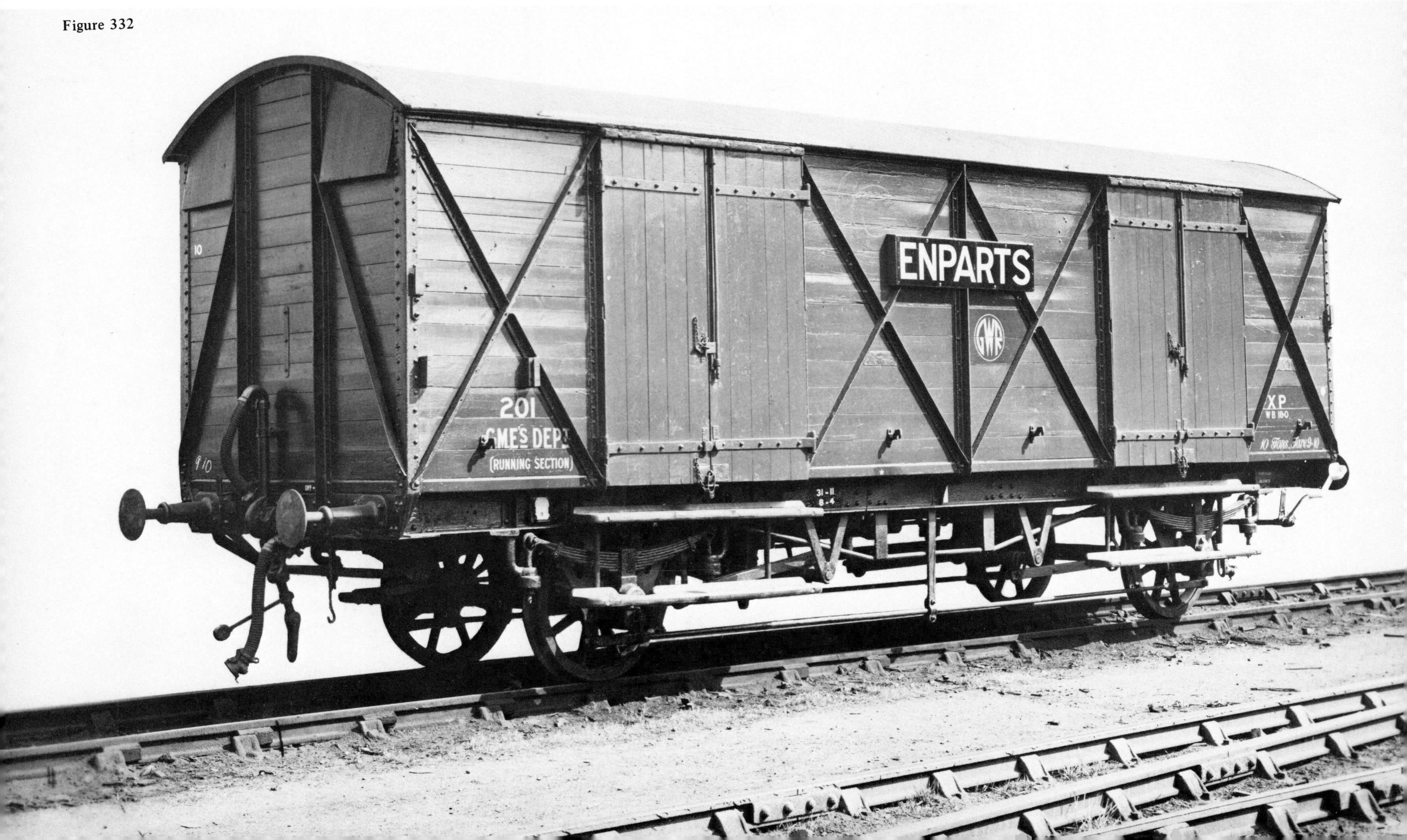

Figure 333

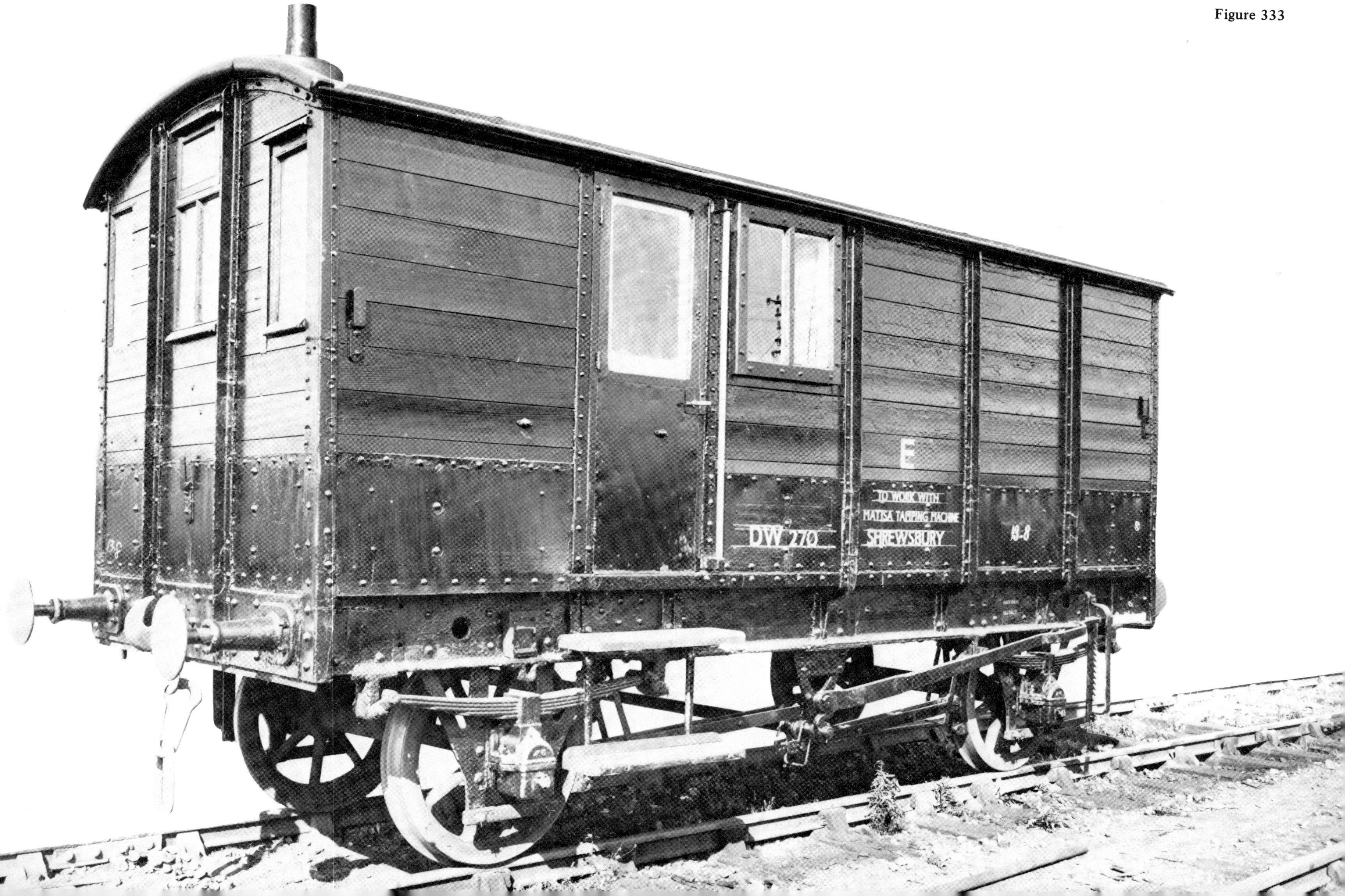

The vehicle in **Figure 333** (above) was originally a Goods brake van No. 56415 and was rebuilt at Swindon in 1952 as a sleeping and messing van for use with one of the 'MATISA' tamping machines. Note that an outside hand brake has had to be fitted.

Another conversion from a goods brake van is shown in **Figure 334.** This was originally a 20 ton brake built on Lot 211 which in 1952 was rebuilt to act as a tool van for the signal and telegraph department at Fishponds, Bristol.

Figure 334

PONTNEWYNYDD
B 950540
12T
B 950540
12 T
SWINDON 1949
LOT NO 2096

Figure 335

Figure 335. This picture of No. B950540 taken in 1949 records the building of the last of the special goods brake vans for use on the Pontnewynydd incline and with specially inclined roof to allow engine crews, with engine next to the van, to see over to the train in front. It was built to Diagram AA/24.

This large double-ended Permanent Way ballast plough brake van seen in **Figure 336** was built at Swindon in 1953. The number was DB993708 and the vehicle was branded 'Return to Menheniot'.

Figure 336

DW 249
ED
17.3
L.22.5.52
R.22.5.52

Another conversion from a goods brake van is shown in **Figure 337** (above). This old vehicle has been fitted with a false flat roof which is capable of being walked upon, and at each end a wooden loading gauge is attached which has a limited 'raise' and 'fall' movement. All this apparatus was for the use of the Engineering department when examining the linings of tunnels.

Figure 338 gives another angle on the tunnel inspection van (No. DW249) and note the handrails which extend along the roof and could be raised upwards to act as handrails to the staff standing on the roof.

Figure 338

Figure 339

A page of contrasts. **Figure 339** shows an early ballast wagon belonging to the Permanent Way Dept., No. 14158, one of many hundreds built to Diagram P2 in 1899 whilst **Figures 340** and **341** illustrate No. DB554633 one of the Rail, Ballast and Sleeper wagons of British Rail, code named 'STURGEON' and pictured by the Western Region in 1953.

Figure 340

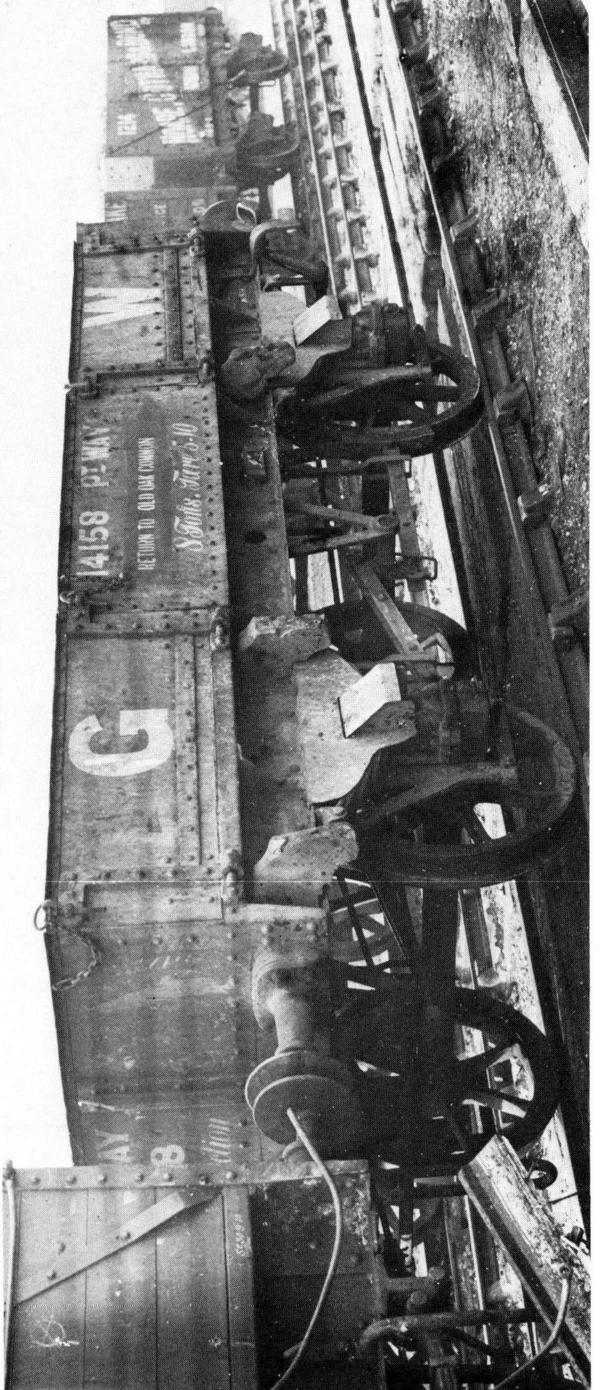

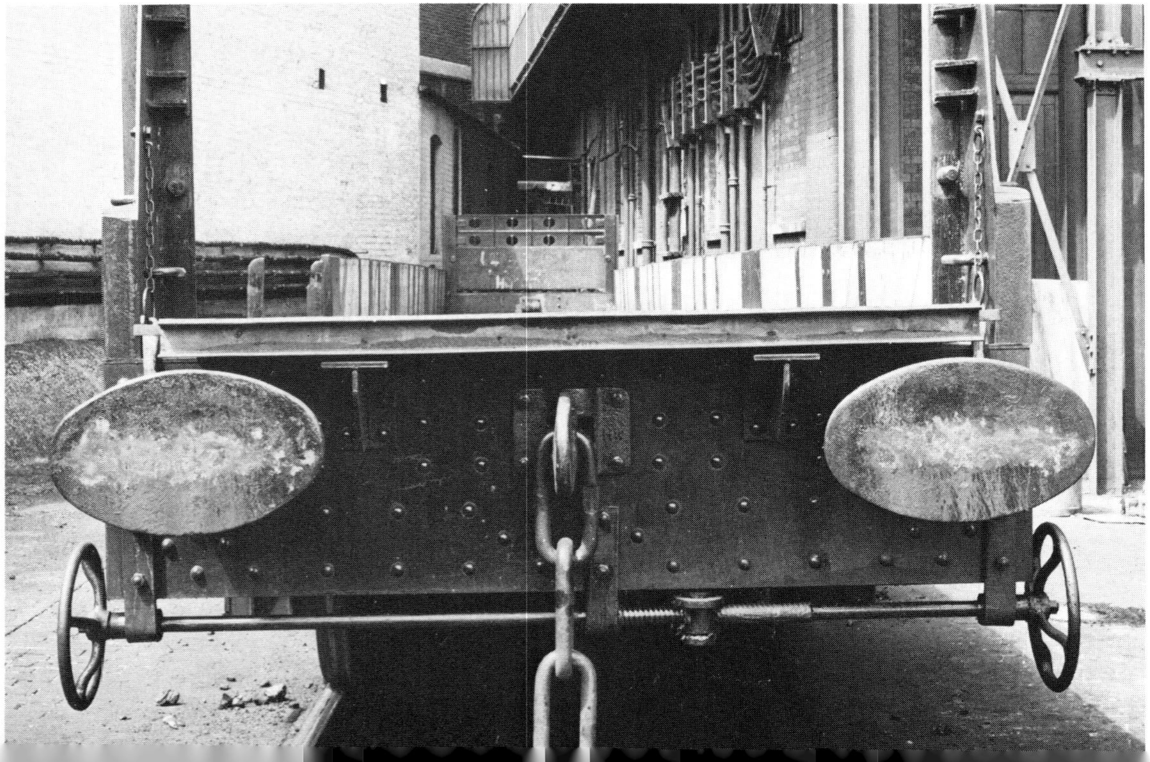

Figure 341

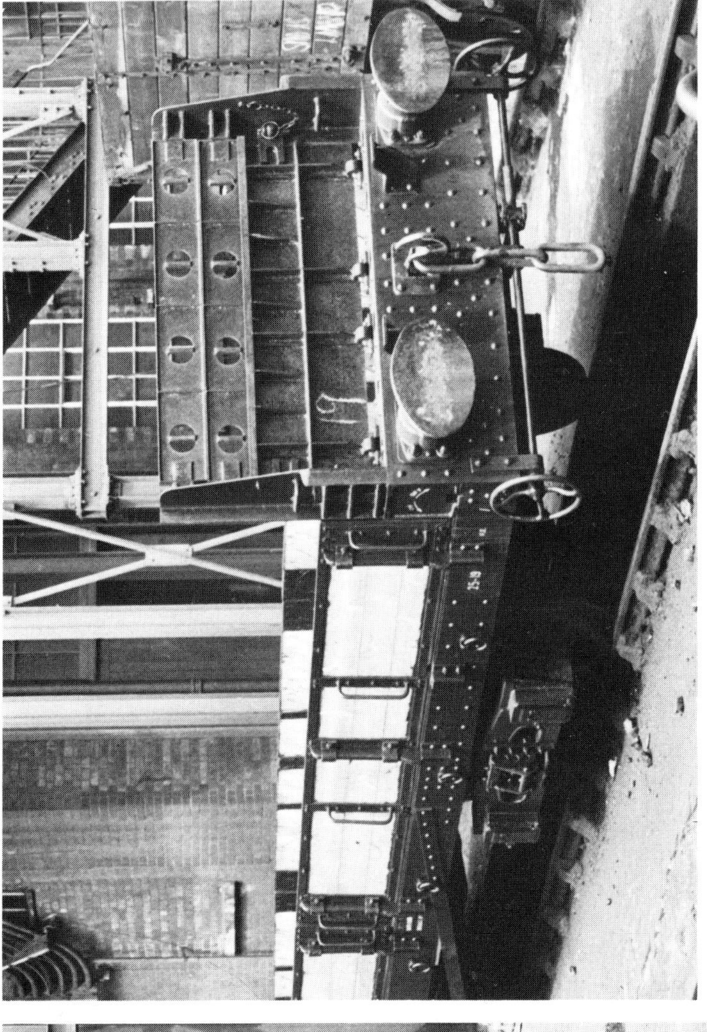

Having illustrated in this work the wide diversity of merchandise carried on the Great Western Railway and British Rail Western Region over the years, this page and the next show the change in the conveyance of that most basic of loads, coal.

Figure 342 taken at Neath in 1912 gives some idea of the volume of the traffic from the Welsh collieries, the majority of which was transported in 'Private Owner' wagons. This picture records how every available siding was filled to capacity with loaded coal wagons. This must have been a great sight for 'wagon' enthusiasts.

Figure 343. In the early 1930s, Sir Felix J. Pole instigated the use of the 20 ton steel coal wagon to replace the ubiquitous 10 and 12 ton wooden coal wagons belonging to or on loan to, thousands of private coal merchants all over the United Kingdom. The idea was to reduce the number of wagons in the coal trains and also to replace the old privately-built wagons, many of which had axles running in grease axleboxes. In the event, however, coal merchants did not take up the option as the new wagons were too big for their small individual loading, the exception being several of the Welsh collieries such as 'Ocean', 'Ebbw Vale' etc.

Figure 344 illustrates today's system of coal wagons, the 'merry go round' trains of large hoppers feeding the power stations at Didcot and Aberthan. These trains enter the sidings and at 4 m.p.h., do not stop; emptying their loads whilst still moving.

Figure 343

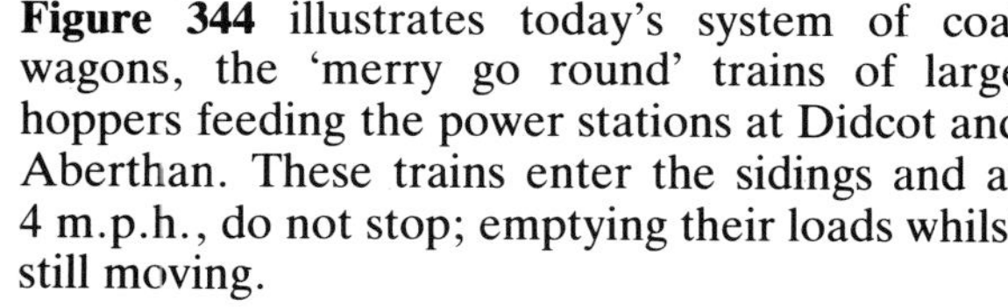

Figure 344

Figure 345

The old and the new in bogie bolster wagons. **Figure 345** taken at Newport Docks in 1926 shows three 'MACAWS B' loaded with steel tubes for export. The numbers of the two bogie vehicles nearest the camera are 84445 and 84599, and the two 'MATCH' wagons acting as runners are Nos. 32234 and 32037.
Figure 346 illustrates the modern equivalent of the Great Western Railway 'MACAW'. This is one of the 'BOGIE STEEL AB' of British Rail, built in 1972 and numbered 900000.

Figure 346

Figure 347

Figure 348

Three photographs of modern 'CARFLAT' wagons built at Swindon by British Rail for the Morris Cowley car traffic at Oxford. **Figure 347** is of No. B748237, a 10 ton Flat vehicle with wheel chocks only, no side rails or drop ends built in 1962 on Lot 3283. **Figure 348** shows a similar vehicle, but with side rails and drop ends. No. B748655 was also built in 1962 on Lot 3358. **Figure 349** records No. B745601 constructed on Lot 3536 in 1964 and fitted with British Rail bogies.

Figure 349

Figure 350

Figure 350 depicts a very special wagon built at Swindon in 1963. This is No. B900524, code named 'FLATROL MJ' and designed expressly for the carriage of atomic flasks. Note the use of roller bearings and compensated axleboxes. Also rebuilt in 1963 is the 'STRIP COIL' bogie vehicle seen in **Figure 351.** This was converted from a 50 ton bogie bolster and the running number was W160250.

Figure 351

Finally on this last page, two very unusual vehicles which were built by British Rail and saw service on the Western Region.

Figure 352 illustrates a 'TIERWAG', a bogie wagon which was designed to carry motor cars on two levels by means of a top deck which could be raised or lowered electrically to accommodate the varying heights of the road vehicles transported. (Note the Great Western Railway style of heavy axleboxes.)

Figure 353 is a rare photograph of that strange vehicle, the 'Diesel Brake Tender'. No. DE320923 was simply an extra source of braking power for use with diesel locomotives and heavy trains. Coupled next to the locomotive, this load of 35 tons with brakes on every wheel of the old Gresley bogies, just gave that little extra stopping power to the lighter of the diesel freight locomotives with their trains of 'non' braked stock.

Figure 352

Figure 353

INDEX

INDEX

INDEX

INDEX

INDEX

INDEX

NOTES

NOTES